# JOURNEY TO
# SAME-SEX
# PARENTHOOD

# JOURNEY TO
# SAME-SEX
# PARENTHOOD

Firsthand Advice, Tips and Stories
from Lesbian and Gay Couples

# ERIC ROSSWOOD

## FOREWORD BY MELISSA GILBERT
## INTRODUCTION BY CHARLIE CONDOU

NEW HORIZON PRESS
Far Hills, New Jersey

Requests for permission should be addressed to:
New Horizon Press
P. O. Box 669
Far Hills, NJ 07931

Eric Rosswood
Journey to Same-Sex Parenthood:
    Firsthand Advice, Tips and Stories from Lesbian and Gay Couples

Cover design: Samantha LemMon
Interior design: Scribe Inc.
Author photo: Beki Dawn Photography

Library of Congress Control Number: 2015913633

ISBN-13 (pb): 978–0-88282–514–4
ISBN-13 (eBook): 978–0-88282–515–1

New Horizon Press

Manufactured in the U.S.A.

20    19    18    17    16        1    2    3    4    5

# What People Are Saying About
## *Journey to Same-Sex Parenthood*

"*Journey to Same-Sex Parenthood* will lead you through moments of both laugh-out-loud humor and immense heartache. This book is informative, emotionally compelling and a must-read for LGBTQ people considering parenthood."

—Zach Wahls
Author of the national bestseller
*My Two Moms: Lessons of Love, Strength, and What Makes a Family*

"Like many other LGBT people, I was desperate to be a parent. I wish *Journey to Same-Sex Parenthood* had been available when I began my own process. It's a fantastic read, filled with beautiful firsthand experiences of becoming families and, to my mind, the ultimate resource for any LGBT person wanting to be a parent."

—Charlie Condou
Actor, Writer, Father and Activist

"This book is an eye-opener for what same-sex couples really go through when trying to start a family. In my work as a legislator advocating on behalf of our community, I've seen the stumbling blocks many couples face on the path to becoming parents—both in law and in society—and this book is a great resource for couples considering this often difficult process."

—NY State Assembly Member Daniel J. O'Donnell
Sponsor of New York's Marriage Equality Act and the state's ground-breaking anti-bullying legislation, the Dignity for All Students Act.

"The resources available to same-sex couples wanting to have children are limited, but *Journey to Same-Sex Parenthood* helps fill that void. The couples in this book have sacrificed their privacy and personal lives to make this road less traveled easier and brighter for future families. This is a must-read for anyone considering adoption."

—Tania Bradkin
Commissioner of Social Services for the City of Santa Monica

"Raising a child is one of the most rewarding experiences we can have, but for same-sex couples, the countless possibilities for starting a family can be overwhelming. *Journey to Same-Sex Parenthood* does a great job when it comes to breaking everything down, comparing all the options and helping readers figure out which path is right for them. I'm so happy a resource like this is available!"

—Judy Appel
Executive Director, Our Family Coalition

# Table of Contents

# DEDICATION

*To my parents, Doyle and Bonnie Ross, for putting up with five boys
and showing us what family is really about; my husband, Mat,
for the love and support you've given me throughout this adventure;
Stephanie and Josh for helping us start a family of our own and our
son, Connor, for giving me inspiration and motivation in life.*

*Also, I want to thank everyone who shared their
personal stories, experiences and advice with me.
Without all of you, this book would not have been possible.*

# Foreword

## by Melissa Gilbert

*New York Times* best-selling author,
wife, mother, actor and activist

Several years ago, I found myself reliving key moments of my life as I started to piece together stories for my memoir. As with most people in the world, my life has been filled with plenty of ups and downs. Through it all, the one thing that stood out to me was the reoccurring theme of family. And when I say family, I don't just mean the nuclear type with a mom, a dad, two-and-a-half kids and a white picket fence. I mean the kind of family built on love, where people are there for each other through thick and thin no matter what happens in life.

This theme dates back to my father, who was an only child and lived with his parents in Philadelphia before being sent away when he was about eight or nine years old. He went to live with a family of circus performers and learned how to be an aerialist like his mother. After both of his parents died when he was just a teenager, he wound up traveling in a circus with his surrogate family.

As for me, I was adopted when I was just a few days old and am the oldest of three children. My mother loved and cherished me the best she knew how and for that I will always love her unconditionally. My father was funny, smart, handsome, kind, generous and fair. He was the kind of parent I aspired to be.

When I was just nine years old, I landed the role of Laura Ingalls Wilder on *Little House on the Prairie*. The cast and crew quickly became my second family and there was a sense of compassion, faith, togetherness, support and camaraderie with everyone on the set. I was particularly close to Michael Landon, an amazing man who was a father figure to me, both on and off screen. He was warm and nurturing and he had a powerful impact on my life. We were so close that my family even had a yearly tradition of going on vacation with Michael and his family.

Flash forward many years and I now have a family of my own, complete with four grown boys, two grown stepsons, a stepdaughter and a granddaughter. My own family includes my dearest friends and their children as well. I am so blessed. I tell people I don't have a family tree, I have a family shrub!

Looking back on my life, my family has been ever-changing. It's been filled with a diverse group of people. What I've learned over the years is that families are strong units that aren't held together by biology; they're held together by love.

Families look different now than they did a few decades ago. Whether they consist of a mother and father, two mommies, two daddies, single parents, a foster family, grandparents or whatever, it's not about what the family looks like. It's about how much they love one another.

Being a parent is the most rewarding thing I will ever do in my life. If it is something you want, I pray your dreams of parenting come true. Every child deserves to be raised in a stable home with parents who love him or her.

I've read and have been touched by all the stories in this book. The lengths that people have gone through to build their families amazes me. I hope their stories help you along in your journey to parenthood.

# Introduction

## by Charlie Condou

### Actor, Writer, Father and Activist

When I came out to my family, they were wonderful about it and it wasn't an issue. There's one thing my mum said to me, though, that I'll always remember: "I feel so sad for you, because you always wanted to be a parent."

To be honest, I *had* always wanted to be a dad and it never crossed my mind that I wouldn't be able to have kids. I didn't know how I was going to start a family, but I just assumed I would.

I was raised in a liberal household and came out to my family when I was eighteen years old. It was the early 90s and a very different time back then. I never saw examples of same-sex couples raising children together and there were no gay parent role models to look up to on TV or in the media. Had I seen other gay men in loving relationships, building families together, it would have removed a lot of fear from my teenage years and made my path to self-acceptance smoother.

My mother loved my sister and me ferociously and has always been supportive of us both. After I came out to her, though, my perspective on family building changed. I could no longer assume that having children was something that would eventually just happen when the right person came along. It would be a little more complicated than that. There was no clear path for me to follow.

At the time, surrogacy was still in its infancy (not to mention extremely expensive) and gay men in the UK were still considered too deviant to adopt. I realized that same-sex couples had to plan more than most people, but it's hard to see how that could be considered a bad thing. My sister told me, "When something is this important to you, you'll find a way."

She was right.

When I was in my thirties, my friend Catherine and I had the "insurance policy" conversation that many gay men have with their female friends: "If we're still single by the time we're forty, we should have kids together." Things were different with Catherine, though. This time the conversation was more serious. We discovered that we had the same morals and same ideals in regards to child rearing.

I eventually met my husband back in 2005. Over the next couple of years, the conversations about having children became more real. We discussed every aspect in regards to what our three-way co-parenting relationship would look like, considered every worst-case scenario we could think of and shared our plans with our families. Everyone was on board and after three cycles of in vitro fertilization (IVF), we had our first positive pregnancy test.

Even though Catherine's house was not far from ours, we all agreed it would be best if she moved in with us for the last bit of the pregnancy and stayed for the first three months after the baby arrived. It turns out that a third pair of hands made a huge difference when our daughter was finally born! We never had to worry about one of us not getting enough sleep, because someone was always there to step in and help. We were able to take turns pacing up and down to comfort our colicky baby and it always seemed that one of us had enough energy to do household chores like making dinner.

We now have two children; one is six years old and the other is three and a half. As parents, we have our own separate lives and our children split the days of the week between both households, but we also make the time to go on holidays, celebrate Christmas and eat meals together as a family. Our arrangement might look unusual to some people but, for our family, it's wonderful because we're all so close.

I think the reason our family situation works so well is that we're upfront and open about everything. We listen to each other and make sure that situations and scenarios work for everyone involved. For those of you wanting to start a family of your own, I think those things are key. Be really clear on what it is you want to do and talk as much as you can. You can never have too many discussions. Talk about worst-case scenarios. What would you do if this happened? What would you do if that happened? Also, be open to change, because even though you may think you have thought of every scenario beforehand, chances are that when your child is eventually born, he or she will just turn all your well-thought-out plans upside down anyway.

Regardless of how you decide to expand your own family, this book is a great resource to help you get started and it provides valuable information to help you along the way. It's a fantastic read and I wish it had been available when I began my own journey. In my mind, it's the ultimate resource for any LGBT person wanting to be a parent and I hope you enjoy reading it as much as I did. Good luck to you. I wish you the best as you begin your own journey to parenthood and enter the next wonderful stage of your life!

# Preface

Marriage equality has been expanding across the globe at a rapid pace and on June 26, 2015, the Supreme Court of the United States ruled that same-sex marriage was legal in all fifty states. You know what they say: First comes love, then comes marriage, then comes a baby in a baby carriage!

As lesbian, gay, bisexual and transgender relationships become more accepted, so do LGBT family units. The Williams Institute, UCLA School of Law, released research in 2013 showing that an estimated three million LGBT individuals have likely had a child and that 2 percent of Americans (roughly six million people) had an LGBT-identified parent. Now that marriage equality is legal throughout the country, these numbers will likely increase as more LGBT people come to the understanding that getting married, settling down and raising a family are obtainable goals and not just dreams.

When my husband and I decided to expand our family, we started evaluating the best way to move forward. We didn't realize researching the topic would be so difficult and time-consuming. There were many choices for same-sex parents looking to have children; however, it was almost impossible to know about them all, let alone research them. What was an open adoption and how was it different from adoption in general? What was co-parenting? These were terms I had never heard of before.

While researching various methods and contacting different agencies, we eventually found the answers to many of our questions regarding costs, processes and legal issues. Lacking, however, were firsthand stories from people who had children themselves. What was it like for the people who went through the process?

I wanted answers to questions like: In an open adoption, how much birthparent contact is typical? If we went with surrogacy, should one of us provide the sperm so there would be a biological connection? And if we went that route, would there be feelings of guilt or resentment revolving around the fact that one of us would be genetically related to the baby and the other one wouldn't be? If we went with foster care, what were the chances that a child would be removed from our home to go back with his or her original parents/guardians after we bonded with him or her? Would fostering be too difficult emotionally?

Sure, a few books exist out there where people have discussed their experiences, but all I could find were single books talking about one way to have a child from one person's point of view. I wanted multiple avenues and multiple points of views in one place.

In the end, we moved forward with an open adoption. It was an amazing journey but, when reflecting back on it, I still wish we had more information going into the scenario. Because of this, I decided to create a resource for potential LGBT parents so they could learn from the experiences of others who had children through similar means. I sought out same-sex couples who had children and asked if they would share their stories on how they became parents. The number one response I got back from people was "Wow, I wish I had something like this when we were going through the process!" And so this book was born.

*Journey to Same-Sex Parenthood: Firsthand Advice, Tips and Stories from Lesbian and Gay Couples* is a resource filled with short stories from people in the LGBT community describing the journey of expanding their families through various means, such as adoption, fostering, surrogacy, assisted reproduction and co-parenting. It is my hope that after reading this book, you will have a better understanding of the thoughts, emotions and situations that may occur in the journey to becoming a parent and get insightful information not necessarily revealed through agencies and organizations.

This book is divided into sections to make it easy for you to quickly research and evaluate the scenarios you are most interested in. To help you in your decision, each section begins with a description of a specific family-building approach, followed by personal stories from same-sex couples who have already been through the journey.

In the appendix section, you will find important legal issues to consider and lists of questions you should ask yourself before deciding to move forward. Hopefully these questions will help you consider things you haven't thought about beforehand and, if nothing else, if you and your partner answer them together they will help make sure you are both on the same page. There is also a list of reasons why people may choose each of the five family-building paths and the challenges they may encounter along the way.

I hope you find this resource helpful and I wish you the best in your own journey to parenthood!

# PART 1
# OPEN ADOPTION

In the past, adoption used to be secretive. No contact was made between the adopting and biological parents and no information was exchanged between them, either. Adopted children grew up without the knowledge of who their birthparents were and, because of this, many grew up believing they were thrown away or given up. A massive transformation occurred when adoptees started demanding the right to know their biological backgrounds and birthmothers started calling for change. Now, open adoption has become the norm for infant adoptions in the United States.

Open adoption was designed as a way to benefit everyone involved, giving all parties (the birthparents, the adoptive family and the child) more information about each other. With open adoption, the birthparents and the adoptive parents meet each other prior to the adoption taking place. They share information with each other and can remain in contact over the years.

This may sound like an awkward scenario at first: Why would you want to remain in contact with the birthparents? Wouldn't that create an uncomfortable situation for everyone involved? It may seem scary, but there are actually numerous benefits to open adoption. Some examples include birthparents having the peace of mind of knowing their child is being raised in a safe and stable home, the adoptive family getting more information about their child's family medical history and the child having the opportunity to know more about his or her biological heritage and background.

The journey begins when the birthmother (and birthfather, if he is still in the picture) decides to place their child for adoption. After contacting an agency and completing an intake session with a counselor, the birthparents choose the adoptive family they want to place their child with.

How do adoptive parents get selected by birthparents? After deciding on an agency, adoptive families complete thorough background checks consisting of mounds of paperwork, medical physicals, fingerprinting, credit checks, home studies, reference checks and more. Once approved by the agency, adoptive families create a "Dear Birthmother" letter. The purpose of this letter is to give birthparents more information about you and to convey how you will raise their child if you are chosen. A simple online search will show you numerous examples of various Dear Birthmother letters. Once completed, the agency sends the letters to various birthparents and the adoptive parents wait to be contacted. It's a bit like online dating. You fill out your profile and wait for the perfect match to contact you.

There's no telling how long your wait might last. You may get contacted right away or you may be waiting for years. While there are things you can do to increase your chances of getting chosen (check with your agency or lawyer since laws are different in each state), the timeline is really left up to fate. The lack of control and unknown future can be very stressful and can even take a toll on your relationship with your partner. Open communication and support for each other is key here.

After the birthfamily chooses an adoptive family and everyone agrees to move forward, they will meet in person and will most likely create what is referred to as a birth plan. This is where you decide things like who will be present during the birth, who holds the baby first and who cuts the umbilical cord. The birth plan is not a contract, but when the birthmother finally goes into labor, it will be used as a guide to help the day run as smoothly as possible.

With open adoption, the birthparents release all of their parental rights and responsibilities, but different states have different laws regulating timelines for when this can happen. They also have different waiting periods for when you can return home if you have an out-of-state adoption. Your agency or attorney can help ensure all criteria are met and the necessary paperwork is filed on time.

Becoming a parent can be a hectic and nerve-racking experience. Some challenges that are common to the open adoption path include unpredictable waiting periods, emotional stress, adoption scams and the possibility that a match will fall through. A qualified and reputable adoption agency can help alleviate some of the stress by weeding out potential scams and providing emotional support to help you get through the challenges that pop up along the way. This support could come in the form of a counselor or support group filled with other families in the same situation as you, sharing their experiences with each other.

This portion of the book will give you insight into what it's like for same-sex couples going through the open adoption journey, while also touching on the many emotional complexities that people have come face-to-face with along the way.

What types of challenges do same-sex couples encounter when trying to obtain a birth certificate for their newborn? What is it like to actually go through a home study? What kinds of adoption scams are out there and what does it feel like to go through one? You'll find the answers to these questions, and many more, after reading this section.

# Mat and Eric Rosswood

BAY AREA, CALIFORNIA

On July 25, 2013, at 5:02 P.M., one sound changed me forever: the first breath of a new life. We had just walked through the door of a midwestern hotel room, not a moment too soon or too late. Our son was finally here.

Becoming a parent wasn't something that generally came up in conversation, even with my best friends. In 2011, as our wedding day approached, I joked that I couldn't possibly have a child outside of marriage—a reference to the ironies of the marriage equality debate more than anything else. Little did we know that soon after that magical day, Eric and I would indeed begin our journey to parenthood.

It still feels strange to talk about "options" when it comes to being a parent—one of many things that provoked unexpected feelings from the start. That's not what they teach you in sex-ed class, but that was our reality and we reflected on them all. Adoption became our choice (a much better word) for two reasons: we would both be equal parents and it felt like the most selfless path to us. I wondered what the world would think of the choice—something I seldom cared about in my general journey through life. Was I really ready to be "that family"?

In June of 2011, we decided to find out and attended an information session at a nearby adoption agency. Every combination of family was present and, while we weren't the only same-sex couple, we were not in the majority. But everyone was there for the same reason and that had a way of making the differences between us seem not so different after all.

As the session evolved, I realized that the other people in the room were about to embark on the same journey that we were. We all had the same goal and I started to think of them as competition. Did any of them have traits or characteristics that would help them match with a birthmother before we did? Instead of thinking about how we could match in the quickest way possible, I started thinking about how we could match before everyone else. How could we "win"? I wasn't ready for that feeling, either. I found it uncomfortable that we saw others in the room as competition and not as comrades who could help each other out. Apparently this is a common feeling for adoptive parents, but knowing that didn't make me feel any better.

The first step in the process was a two-day weekend intensive program. "If you are patient and do what we say, you will get a baby," they told us in the opening session. I wondered again how many times I'd feel uncomfortable on this journey. We met our counselor for the first time and left with binders, books and contracts.

As I read through all of the information and started to understand the next steps, I felt another emotion I hadn't expected in our journey to parenthood: anger. Reproduction is part of the natural order of the human race, a right acquired at birth that no law denies, at least in the United States. As I learned of all the hoops we were about to jump through, the thought did cross my mind: I'm a human being and I have the right to reproduce like everyone else. All I needed was a willing human of the opposite sex. Instead, we were about to take one serious parenting test: get fingerprinted, go through a background check by the Federal Bureau of Investigation, have our financials rummaged through, get poked and prodded by a doctor, have our blood tested, provide references and go through an afternoon of interviews, all to become parents to the child of some straight couple who couldn't fulfill the role that the natural order ordained them with. All they did was have some fun. *That* made me angry.

I know our son will read this one day. That is not how I think of his biological mother or father. I also know the beauty that is life can come from some truly harrowing circumstances, but at that moment, I was indeed mad at those who just "did it" without a care in the world or a questionnaire and then abused or discarded their children, straight or gay.

Then we began to do all of our homework and that anger gave way to a much deeper emotion. I felt like a normal human being—more unexpected feelings. I realized I knew very little about being a parent, something I now know many first-time parents feel. Not that this made filling out the parenting questionnaire any easier. I was trying to answer questions I had never asked myself before: What *is* the difference between discipline and abuse? How *am* I going to talk to our child about sex?

Where does one go to find answers to those questions? In the modern age, online search engines aren't a bad source of inspiration, but there was another place I could go to for expert advice—my own parents. I don't remember when I first told them we were planning to adopt, but we were on a family vacation when I asked them about parenting. We explained all of the things we'd been doing to "qualify" as adoptive parents.

"What did you talk about before I was born?" I asked.

"The only real thing we'd decided beforehand was that we would always be on the same page in front of you, even if we disagreed afterward," my dad said. There was that "normal" feeling again, along with the realization that all of this question asking and book reading was actually helping Eric and I, both individually and together, to prepare to be parents and to think about things we otherwise likely never would have thought about or discussed before. I wasn't so angry anymore.

I've studied for plenty of tests, written plenty of papers and essays and given presentations on all manner of topics, but I was at a loss as to how one prepares for a parent interview. Is there a right answer to a parenting question? Did I say the right things in my biography? Was I too honest or not honest enough? What if my "discipline versus abuse" response wasn't good enough? What if Eric said something different from what I had when he was interviewed or disagreed with me—what would that mean? I figured I would just go with my gut instincts—isn't that what parents do? I didn't know. But that made me no different from any other prospective parent.

We passed the interview. I wondered if people ever failed it but didn't ask. The home study came next. At the time, we lived in a newly-built condominium that we had bought together shortly after our engagement. It suited us perfectly as a couple, although now we needed to make some changes—installing carbon monoxide detectors, buying a fire extinguisher and moving everything potentially harmful to an infant out of reach (even though a newborn couldn't reach it for a number of years). We did everything we were asked to do. It seemed to take forever. Then the envelope finally arrived to say we had passed the tests and were now approved adoptive (and foster) parents. We were excited to be one step closer to becoming dads.

We spent weeks writing and rewriting and designing our Dear Birthmother letter, picking photographs and changing layouts. When it was finished, it looked like four pages from *People* magazine. We thought we had the best letter ever written—more enthusiasm than arrogance—and were convinced we would be picked almost immediately. We finished our online profile with the agency and set up the required e-mail address and 800 number so a birthmother could reach us anytime without cost to her. Then we were all set to start waiting for the call.

We wondered how we would feel when it rang for the first time and didn't have to wait long to find out—about as long as it took us to learn that 800 numbers are recycled and otherwise prone to misdials. The first call I excitedly picked up was someone trying to get her cell phone fixed. These numbers also seem to get easily placed on automated call lists, so the phone rang at all hours, day and night. Each time we hoped it was "the call," only to usually find no one on the other end of the line. Then we would wonder whether we should call the number back in case it was a birthmother trying to reach us, even though the agency told us not to call the birthmothers back—and for good reason. If the birthmother hadn't told anyone about her pregnancy, you didn't want to accidently unveil her secret if another family member answered when you called back.

Eric and I had said at the beginning of our journey that we were going to try to live a normal life during the wait. The agency told us the same thing and discouraged "nesting" or anything nursery-related before placement. For six months, nothing really happened, so we decided to try some new things. Eric started a few social media accounts while I tried my hand at website design. We talked about redesigning "The Best Dear Birthmother Letter Ever," which had only been sent out once, and about whether we wanted to change our client profile.

The client profile sets out the adoptive family's preferences regarding the birthparents' racial heritage and religious background. It also specifies the behaviors they find tolerable in regard to smoking, drinking and drug use during pregnancy, as well as the level of physical and mental disability we would accept. Of all the forms we had to fill out, that one was by far the hardest. We were told that the more "liberal" we were on the form, the greater the chance of us being shown to a birthmother who had contacted the agency. We'd done a lot of reading on drinking and drugs—many of the people I know seem to have some form of fetal alcohol syndrome, the symptoms of which include being grumpy and angry—and so we weren't too particular about those boxes. When it came to hereditary medical history, however, things started to get more complex.

Consider this question: If you could choose between an unimpaired child or a physically or mentally challenged child, which would you choose? Biological parents don't have that choice, whereas adoptive parents do (to some degree, because nothing is ever certain). So what choice do you make and does it show you as a good or bad parent in the eyes of a birthmother? The options available on the form are not extensive: no condition, a mild condition of any type or any condition. Eric and I both have or have had close relatives with mental impediments. Would we pick a child with a mental impediment or a notable risk of one if we had the choice? What would we do if our child was born with an otherwise undiagnosed physical or mental impediment? Adoptions can be "broken" at any point before they are finalized by either party. Would we ever consider doing that? We talked about it for a long time, agreeing that the universe would grant us whatever it did. So we checked the "mild" box and entered the adoption pool.

After six months of nothing, I did start to wonder whether we had made the right choices on the form and whether we should have checked another box or two. It was around that time when we got our first e-mail. It arrived at about 11:30 P.M. one night. We both had our adoption e-mail address synced to our phones and so far had only received random junk mail. But this time, our devices went "ping" and it was a birthmother. We were excited, apprehensive and eager to respond, so we jumped out of bed to reply—and then realized we had no idea what to say! It probably took us two hours to draft a two-paragraph message, redraft it, bicker a little about what we were going to write, redraft it some more and finally send it. Then we forwarded our reply to the adoption agency and tried to get some sleep, wondering all the while if we had said the right things and when she would reply, if she ever would.

Two e-mails later, we realized we were being scammed. The person was just trying to get money from us. We had been warned several times that this could and would likely happen. Knowing how raw and vulnerable adoptive parents are during "the wait," it's hard to imagine how a decent human being could prey on that, but people do. One of the many benefits of working with an agency is that they are very quick to spot a scam and let us know before we become too emotionally invested. To be fair, though, after a six-month wait and a sleepless night writing perhaps the most important e-mail of our lives, we were up to our ears in emotional investment and it was hard not to be a little sad that this wasn't the one.

We put it behind us, along with a few other scams among the random calls we got. Before we knew it, one year had passed and we became eligible for the "last-minute list." This meant we would be one of the families presented to a birthmother who decided to place immediately after birth. If she liked us, we would have thirty minutes to decide if we wanted to move forward. We tried to make that the positive outcome of a year spent waiting—we could now become a family instantaneously—and signed up.

Five days later, my cell phone rang while I was in a meeting at work. It was a number my phone didn't recognize, so I ignored it. When I got home, we had a voicemail I hadn't noticed earlier. It was around 9:30 P.M. when I pushed play in the kitchen and, after a moment of silence, we heard Stephanie's voice for the first time.

"Hi, Eric and Mat…" There was a long pause. "Wow, this is awkward. My name is Stephanie. I saw your profile online. I'm thirteen weeks pregnant and I'm looking to place my baby for adoption. And I really liked your profile and would kinda like to get to know more about your parenting style and things like that. If you could please give me a call, I look forward to talking more with you."

This was real and now it was our turn to be silent. From her phone number, we deduced that she was in the central time zone, so it was past 11 P.M. and had been almost twelve hours since her call. *Do we call her back now? Do we wait until the morning? What would she be thinking?*

*What do we say to her when we call? What are we supposed to do?* We decided to send a text—that way she would know we got her message when she woke up. Stephanie replied in about fifteen seconds. After a brief exchange of texting small talk, we called her.

Our first call lasted close to two hours. We told her to ask us anything she wanted to know. She started with our views on pediatric vaccinations and circumcision. We were not prepared at all to start there, but were honest and answered every question she had as best we could. I took lots of notes. By the time the call ended, we were overwhelmed and could only imagine how she felt. Of all the things we covered that night—the fact that she was declared medically infertile after the birth of her second child, the night the baby was conceived (Halloween, Eric's favorite holiday), her family situation, her decision not to terminate, her desire to have a home birth and her disdain for adoption agencies—the one that sticks in my mind the most is the response she gave to our question, "What drew you to us when you read our profile?" Stephanie said that she is a Capricorn and her best friend is a Libra. Since I'm a Capricorn and Eric is a Libra, she took that as a sign. The stars really were shining on us that day and they all seemed to be pointing towards Stephanie being the one.

The following day, we had another long conversation with Stephanie over video chat and met the birthfather, Josh. We all seemed to get on well, cracking jokes and laughing and getting to know each other. We gave Stephanie the number for our adoption agency and e-mailed our adoption coordinator to tell her about the contact, hoping we were not in fact seeing stars and that this was for real.

Eric and I spent much of Sunday discussing everything we had learned about Stephanie and Josh. We counted the weeks from thirteen to thirty-nine and tried not to think about the twenty-six weeks during which she could change her mind. We also tried to fathom how a non-hospital birth would work. Stephanie told us she had recently separated from her husband (not Josh) and was currently living in a shelter with her two children. Even though her living situation was complex, Stephanie did not want a hospital birth, which left us with the big overhanging question: "How do you have a home birth without a home?"

Monday came around and we called the agency to fill them in. Stephanie called them later that week and started the intake process and pregnancy validation. Like I said, the agency doesn't pull any punches when it comes to ensuring their families are not being scammed.

Eric and I had agreed not to tell anyone about the call until we knew for certain that we were going to move forward—it was the hardest secret we've ever kept. Every call to our respective parents (and to everyone who knew of our family plans, for that matter) always included some reference or question about the adoption and whether there was any news. We told them not to ask, but couldn't blame them for asking, either. We appreciated everyone's questions and concerns, particularly our parents, who tried very hard to understand how the whole process was going to work. After all, they were as novice to this journey as we were, despite being grandparents already. We didn't want to jinx anything, so we waited until the match meeting was confirmed before we told them about the call.

Our first meeting was scheduled for February 13 in Stephanie's hometown, which was a good 1,800 miles away from us. We flew in the day before and she met us at the airport at 10:45 P.M.—you may note that she's a night owl. We had spoken a number of times since that first call and texted incessantly, but we were still nervous as all hell when we met in person for the first time. Before us was the impossible dream and it could have been shattered in a heartbeat if we had done something wrong. And there was no way of really knowing what "wrong" might have been. We made our way through checking into a hotel and having dinner without her leaving, so we hoped we were on the right track as we arranged to meet again in the morning.

I never expected to feel pregnant as part of the adoption and had no idea what that would even feel like. I don't mean cravings (even though I've now tried pickles with whipped cream and it's totally gross), morning sickness, backaches or sleepless nights, although somehow Eric and I managed to gain a sympathetic fifteen pounds each and we have been working it off ever since. I mean the pre-natal journey itself. We had expected to match with someone much more advanced in her pregnancy—maybe six months along—and really not be that involved. But there we were, standing in an ultrasound technician's laboratory at the hospital, watching the monitor and learning we were having a baby boy. I had never expected to have that experience.

The match meeting took place at our hotel later that morning. It was facilitated by not one, but two adoption agencies: one from our home state of California and one from Stephanie's home state of Illinois. Together, we all started to talk about a birth plan and post-adoption contact. There were a lot of forms to be filled out and the "transactional" feeling in those moments still makes me uncomfortable. The end result, though, was a successful match! And all too soon, it was time to fly back to California. We were elated and scared to death.

We spoke with Stephanie about once a week after that and swapped endless text messages. We've printed many of the early ones so our son can read them for himself one day. It was difficult to know just how much contact we should have with Stephanie at that point. We didn't want to overwhelm her by texting, calling or e-mailing too much, but on the other hand, we didn't want her to feel like we weren't very interested. Sometimes a day or two passed between messages and we silently hoped that the pause was just another day in the busy life of a single mom of two, rather than a change of heart. Then another message from her came, along with a deep sigh of relief.

I had buried my head in the sand about the home birth for three months, hoping that Stephanie might change her mind or the agency would require a hospital so I wouldn't have to think about it again. That ostrich syndrome was accompanied by a deep-seated fear that, if I couldn't get my head around it and we couldn't make it work, our journey would come to an untimely and unhappy ending. We had to find a way. But how do you arrange a home birth when you don't have a home?

To add to the complexity of the home birth situation, certified nurse midwives are required to have a signed collaborative agreement with an obstetrician in order to practice in Illinois. For some reason, that is extremely difficult to get and doesn't happen often. The result is an under-ground group of midwives unofficially performing home births, which doesn't really work for an adoption where everything needs to be official.

Quite the dilemma! So two months before the due date, we got on a plane to figure everything out together. Stephanie had already solved the midwife challenge: Kathleen Devine, a fitting name for the person who was to deliver our gift from the heavens. Kathy lived about an hour from Stephanie in the neighboring state of Iowa and was thrilled to be a part of our journey. The only catch was that we now had to cross the state line to give birth—not that this was getting complicated or anything.

We also still had to solve the "where" of the actual delivery. First we looked at some vacation home rentals, but the neighboring towns were not exactly big vacation destinations. There wasn't much in the way of corporate housing either and we were starting to despair when a friend of Stephanie's suggested the hotel we stayed at when we first visited, which had two-bedroom suites. Stephanie could stay in one bedroom while Eric and I stayed in the other. We toured the rooms that afternoon and booked before we left.

After our rooms were secured, we met up with Julie, our Illinois adoption coordinator, to finalize the birth plan. We went over who was going to be in the room at the time of birth and who was going to hold the baby first. Eric was mostly worried about the noise and mess of the whole thing, since Stephanie was giving birth in a hotel room. But Stephanie reassured us that actual births are less messy than the ones portrayed in movies and on TV. She also said that Kathy would lay out puppy pads to absorb everything and make the clean-up easy. We laughed at the thought of a fully pregnant Stephanie crowning while squatting over puppy pads in a hotel bathroom. It sounded like a comedy series waiting to happen.

"What about the placenta?" Eric asked. It seemed like an odd question, but seeing as the placenta couldn't really be absorbed in a puppy pad, I guess it was a fair one to ask.

"We'll put it in the freezer," Stephanie replied.

"For what?" Eric quipped. "A snack later?"

"Yes," she said matter-of-factly. "We'll dry it out in the oven and use a coffee grinder to grind it into pills." Our eyes widened and our jaws dropped when we realized she wasn't joking. "The nutrients are really good for your body. We can even bake it into a lasagna."

"You mean plasagna?" Eric joked. We all broke up laughing at the table.

Everything was coming together. It was all very real and only two months away. Eric and I owned nothing baby-related at that point. We'd been told all we needed was a change of clothes and a car seat to leave the hospital, but as there was no hospital involved, we had to make up our own rules. We took our first baby-shopping trip and came back with way too much stuff. Everyone else was banned from buying any baby things until three days after he was born.

While it seemed like forever as we lived it day-to-day, the month of the birth arrived before we knew it. We had been capturing potential names for about two years. Eric even bought me a book of 20,000 baby names for my birthday, as if we didn't have enough to choose from already. I had a fantasy when we started the adoption process that our birthmother would let us choose the baby's first name, so that it would match on both of his birth certificates (the one issued at birth and the one issued with our names as the parents after we finalized the adoption).

Reality turned out to be much better than my fantasy. As Stephanie had no attachment to either her married name or her maiden name, she had already decided to give the baby our last name and whatever other names we wanted. For his middle name, we initially thought about asking Stephanie to choose it but, as she had insisted it was our decision, we selected Stephen in her honor. There were a few tears that day. And while everyone around us was getting excited at the pending arrival, we kept his name a secret until three days after he was born.

Having been part of the pregnancy pretty much since the beginning and given the complexities of the birth arrangements, we had planned to fly back to the Midwest ten days prior to our son's due date. We arrived to a very pregnant Stephanie and settled into our hotel suite together—she (and sometimes her two children) in a room at one end and us in a room at the other end. Josh, the birthfather, stopped by and we all took turns guessing the actual arrival date. We were all convinced the birth was imminent. How wrong could we be?

Every morning we woke up, ate breakfast together and politely inquired if there was "any sign of arrival" before going about our day. Every twinge or cringe from Stephanie prompted the same. After ten days, the due date had come and gone and we were all going a little stir-crazy holed up in a hotel room.

At five days late, we all went to see the midwife to find out if the baby was stressed. Thankfully he wasn't, unlike his parents-to-be. Kathy handed Stephanie two capsules containing a specially blended homeopathic labor inducer. We had talked before about induction—Stephanie was very clear that she wanted everything to happen naturally—so this was as close to a natural induction as we could get.

On the way back to the hotel, we picked up some children's paint and spent the evening painting pictures on Stephanie's stomach to have a little fun and relieve some stress before she took the pills, just in case they worked and tomorrow was indeed the *big* day. We all laughed together as we painted a giant sun on her belly, followed by a huge rainbow. When we started this whole adoption journey, we envisioned meeting a birthmother close to her due date and never really imagined having a relationship with her, let alone living with her or painting her giant, pregnant belly. We were really bonding and it felt good. It felt right.

There was no guarantee the labor inducer would work, so when we all got up the following morning to have breakfast and watch Stephanie take the first pill, we figured it would just be another day. Lunchtime came and we called the midwife, who told Stephanie to take the second pill. Within about thirty minutes, Stephanie came back into the living room of our hotel suite. She looked profoundly different and announced the baby was on his way. Stephanie had labored for a day with her previous two children and so when Kathy and her assistant, Monica, arrived an hour later, followed by Josh shortly after that, we figured we were in for a very long night. Wrong again!

At 4:47 P.M., her water broke. Stephanie was in the bathroom and we were at the other end of the suite in our room. She asked that we leave, so Josh, Eric and I took a walk across the street. We were gone about twelve minutes when everyone's phone started to beep and we raced back to the hotel.

Our Connor had finally arrived. We walked into the room the moment he took his first breath and, although we couldn't see him, we heard his first cry. Fortunately, no one had a camera pointed at us at that time—our faces would have made quite the picture.

About thirty minutes later, Kathy came into our room to give us an update. She had a puppy pad for an apron that was covered in blood. So much for there not being a mess! The midwife told us that Connor had gotten stuck on his way into the world. His cord had wrapped around his neck and snapped upon delivery, spraying blood and stem cells all over the bathroom and its occupants. But thanks to Kathy and her quick responsiveness, a life-threatening situation was avoided and everything turned out fine.

Kathy told us that Stephanie was getting settled and that she would come back to get us shortly when Stephanie was ready. To this day, the hotel has no idea what happened in Room 908 that afternoon. If anyone ever takes a blacklight into that bathroom, they will likely call the FBI.

The next thirty minutes felt like forever. When Kathy finally came back into the room to get us, every possible emotion swept over me. Most of all, I just wanted to see him. As we walked across the hall, our hearts in our throats, I wondered how it was going to feel when my eyes met his for the first time. I soon discovered it was like nothing I've ever felt before in my life. There he was, curled up against Stephanie, feeding. We knew he was feeding before we went into the room—it was at the midwife's recommendation to help Stephanie heal physically—but I couldn't stop the feeling of dread that suddenly came over me.

We had discussed long before that there would be no breastfeeding, given the bonding it promoted. This was Stephanie's position and we had supported it. Now I was overcome with doubt that she might change her mind. She smiled as she saw us, looking more beautiful than ever despite being completely exhausted. She motioned for us to come and hold our son. I held him first. I'd never held something so precious in my entire existence, an existence that now felt more complete.

I quickly realized just how instinctive parenting is—although I defy any man to be truly ready to change his first meconium-filled diaper, complete with a birthmother and midwife audience. As we fumbled around, the fear of Stephanie changing her mind about the adoption still lingered in the back of our heads. It had just taken us ten minutes to change a diaper. What if she thought that meant we weren't ready to be parents?

I mentioned earlier about waiting three days before telling everyone the baby's name and a three-day ban on buying gifts, but didn't explain why. Every state has its own adoption laws, including the point at which an adoption can progress after birth. For us, that was three days. The next seventy-two hours were the most complex of the entire process. We were still living in the same hotel room with Stephanie, as we had been for three weeks. Eric and I were in a state of exhausted joy as she began to grieve. It was a humbling irony; there was nothing that could be said, nothing that we could do to fix it or heal it. Of all the unexpected things we had experienced on this journey, those three days were by far the most profound. They made us ever more grateful for Connor as the process reached its conclusion and we could take our son home.

It has been over a year now and we are still in constant contact with Stephanie. We text, phone or video chat once or twice a week. Video chat is wonderful since it allows Connor and Stephanie to see each other and it's an added bonus when Stephanie's two children are able to join in as well. We also have an agreement to meet in person once a year. We just flew back to Illinois recently to see Stephanie, Josh and Josh's mom. We had a wonderful time with plenty of great photo opportunities.

If you were to ask her, Stephanie would tell you that she didn't give Connor to us; she gave *us* to *him* and we are forever blessed that she bestowed that honor upon us. Stephanie is now a part of our family, as we are a part of hers. Although life will take us all in many new and exciting directions, we will be forever bound, because the bond of love between parent and child is the strongest bond of all.

# Chris and Novia Rowzee

CORYDON, INDIANA

When my wife and I met in 2001, she was twenty-three and I was thirty-eight, so obviously we had a fairly significant age gap between us. But she was clearly an "old soul" and I'm perpetually immature, so we sort of met in the middle and it worked for us. One area in which the age difference was clear, though, was in our different points of readiness for children. I was ready to start a family and hoping to meet someone with whom I could build that family. Novia wasn't quite ready for children yet, although she did want a family eventually. She just had other things she wanted to do first. Although I wasn't getting any younger, I hadn't yet hit that unknown age where I would be uncomfortable as a "mom," so we waited. We originally planned on artificial insemination, but knew adoption was also a perfectly acceptable possibility to both of us.

Our lives and relationship were certainly complicated and not just because of our age difference. When we met, I was living in Little Rock and working full time as a Major in the Arkansas Air National Guard. In those days of "Don't Ask, Don't Tell," being a lesbian in my field was downright oppressive. By law, I couldn't be "out" in the military and I lived in constant fear of being outed and losing my job. I had been living in the closet my entire military career, which at that point spanned almost seventeen years.

Novia was also in the military. After we started dating, I convinced her to transfer to the Air National Guard and she was eventually hired into a full-time position in my unit. So there we were, both of us working for the same Guard unit, living in a military town and trying to make a relationship work while avoiding getting drummed out for being gay.

Because of the nature of my position, I was very well-known and recognized by virtually everyone in my eleven-hundred-person unit. Pretty much anywhere I went around town, there'd be people who would recognize me. Novia and I were in constant fear of being seen together. We'd drive to the grocery store on base in different cars and shop separately, starting at opposite ends of the store while talking on our cells to make sure we got what we needed. We'd worry about going out to dinner together or Novia being seen mowing our yard and having people realize that she lived there with me. We struggled with trying to figure out how we might raise a child in that environment.

Then something happened during my deployment to the desert in 2005 that significantly changed our lives and our relationship. Just a couple of months into my six-month deployment, my appendix ruptured and I became very ill, almost septic. That event made me realize I didn't want my entire life centered on hiding who I was and having to hide my family. I realized there was no way we could have the family we wanted if we stayed in the military full time. So we made a huge decision to leave full-time military service and move away.

Now a Lieutenant Colonel, I started job hunting and I eventually landed a federal job with the Department of Veterans Affairs in Louisville, Kentucky. It was a beautiful area, a big enough city where there was lots to do, yet not so big that it was a concrete jungle. I moved there just after Christmas in 2006 and Novia followed me there six months later after also getting a federal job. It wasn't until we moved out of the "fishbowl" existence in which we'd lived for the previous five years that we realized the stress and emotional toll it had taken on us. We felt like we could finally breathe.

Novia and I were able to be more open at our new workplaces and live more authentic lives, so we moved forward with our plans to start a family. We wanted to get settled first, so we built a new house and moved in about a year later. Then the family planning process started in earnest. At that point, we wanted to just go straight to adoption. We ultimately decided against artificial insemination for a couple of reasons: My age was starting to be of concern in carrying a child and Novia had some health issues with childbearing, plus we only had finite resources to use in starting our family. If insemination didn't work, we'd have exhausted them with no child to show for it and no further resources for an adoption. So adoption it was!

As with anything I do, I thoroughly researched everything I could find about adoption, including what types there were and how to go about it. I shared all I learned with Novia. We weren't going to hide our family or pretend this child wasn't going to be raised by two mommies. We thought about foreign adoption, but soon learned that many countries don't allow gay couples (or single women, older women, etc.) to adopt. We also considered adoption through the state foster care system but decided against that, because we really wanted an infant—preferably a newborn—and didn't want to risk getting a child who we would have to give back. I knew myself well enough to know I couldn't stand that. With those constraints, our chances within the state system slimmed down considerably, so we opted for an agency placement approach.

I read everything I could find on how to pick a good agency. I searched for reviews online, sent e-mails and asked for references. There was a good deal to be leery of: a lot of scams are out there, as well as legal pitfalls with potentially disastrous consequences. Again, we couldn't afford to waste resources by making any mistakes. I talked to quite a few agencies and the first question I always asked was: "Do you work with same-sex couples?" I got a variety of answers, from flat out "No" to "Absolutely, we have placed many children with same-sex families" to "Yes, but you'd only be eligible for our African-American program."

It didn't matter to us what race, nationality or ethnicity our child might be: white, African-American, purple or Martian for all we cared! But we were highly offended that an agency believed minority children were somehow less worthy and could "settle for" same-sex parents or that we weren't "good enough" for a white child. I refused to even consider those agencies. Then there were some agencies that left me feeling like it was just a business to them, some sort of "baby transaction."

We finally settled on an agency that we discovered through word of mouth. A gay coworker and his partner had adopted through them twice and described a very accepting environment that was focused on creating loving families. It was a small agency and we liked that aspect. They didn't work with a large number of couples, but being smaller also meant fewer birthmothers coming to them. However, they seemed to have a pretty good success rate and had worked successfully with numerous same-sex couples. So we signed on!

That was when things got complicated. We had built our house and now lived in a small rural town in Indiana, just across the Ohio River from Louisville, Kentucky. But like many in our area, we worked and most often "played" in Louisville. Our adoption agency was located in Louisville as well. Adoption law is state-specific, with each state setting its own rules and requirements. Most states have "agreements" with other states that allow adoptions to occur across state lines, but these are very tightly controlled. Because we lived in Indiana, our home study and all pre-placement requirements had to be conducted by an Indiana agency and conform to Indiana rules. But because we were working with a Kentucky placement agency, we also had to meet Kentucky requirements and follow that state's laws as well. Upon placement, we were not allowed to bring the baby across state lines (even just the few miles to our home) until the state of Kentucky authorized it—and they likely wouldn't do that until they had full termination of parental rights. We were told this could take as long as ninety days. During that time, we could not live in anyone's private residence that was not home study approved, so we would have to stay in a hotel!

I have to admit, it was more than a little daunting to think about trying to care for a newborn baby in a hotel room for three months. But we pressed on with little choice, particularly since we hadn't been able to find a placement agency in Indiana that we were comfortable with. So we began filling out forms and got our fingerprints taken multiple times. We were sent to three different government entities for checks and got letters of recommendation from what seemed like everyone going back to elementary school.

Next, we found an agency to do all of the pre- and post-placement work required by Indiana. We drove two hours to Indianapolis on multiple occasions to take the agency's training and complete the interviews needed for our home study. We wrote ten-page-long biographies of our lives and answered dozens of questions about our relationship and how we envisioned raising a child. We hired someone to create our "profile book," essentially a photo storybook of our lives, interests and home—something a prospective birthmother could look at to get a sense of our family. We found an experienced adoption attorney licensed in both Kentucky and Indiana, since there would be legal actions in both states. And it seemed like every time we turned around, our Kentucky agency discovered something else we needed to do, because of our "dual state" situation.

I can honestly say my top-secret military security clearance seemed easier to obtain than an approved home study and adoption package for the states of Indiana and Kentucky! But finally, FINALLY, we were approved. We started this paperwork and training process in the fall of 2008 and were able to go on the active list in May 2009.

Then the real waiting began. I don't know how to describe waiting for "the phone call" other than you feel like your life is on hold. Do you put the deposit down for that cruise knowing "the call" would cancel those plans? Do you consider a new job or make large expenditures knowing your financial obligations could drastically change at any time? How do you plan your life knowing that, at any moment, it could turn upside down?

So we joined a "While You Wait" support group through our Kentucky placement agency. We shared updates, talked about concerns and just generally provided an outlet for things that most of our friends and family couldn't relate to. There were other same-sex couples in the group, so we weren't alone in that respect, either. It was nice to have that group connection, but at times it was very difficult to participate, especially as the wait became longer. It seemed there was always another new couple joining the group and we felt guilty for viewing them as our competition. Every couple who joined was one more family that a potential birthmother had to choose from.

We were constantly figuring the odds: how many birthmothers the agency told us they were working with against how many waiting families were there in the support group. Each time a family was matched, we were genuinely happy for them, excited they would soon take their child home. At the same time, however, we couldn't help but ask ourselves, "Why not us?" and then later, "What's wrong with us?" After a while it became very disheartening to continue attending the meetings. Then there were moments when we heard the "disruption" stories, about how a match didn't work out for one reason or another. Those always brought tears to everyone's eyes. Our hearts ached for the families and then we prayed it didn't happen to us.

After the first year with no match, Novia and I decided that we just had to get on with our lives. We had to make plans and do things without worrying about "what if" we got a phone call. So we went on a cruise and visited family, all the while making sure the agency knew how to contact us and having contingency plans in the backs of our minds, just in case.

We also started buying baby stuff, the big-ticket items like a crib, dresser, stroller and car seat, all of those things that cost a fortune if you buy them all at once. So every couple of months we picked up something else we knew we'd need. We didn't set up the nursery yet, but we still wanted to make sure we were fairly ready. That way, when the call came, all we had to do was prepare the room.

There was a lot of debate among the members of our group as to whether or not couples should set up a nursery ahead of time. Some families, like ours, were planners and wanted to be ready. Others thought it would be too hard to see that empty nursery every day. Now, I can see both points of view.

For a long time, we really didn't have much luck. Apparently, the poor economy had a pretty devastating effect on the country's birth rate, so there just weren't very many birthmothers coming in. Later, when the traffic did finally pick up, we still weren't getting any interest. Our caseworker became concerned and suggested we revamp our profile book. She thought that maybe it wasn't conveying the right message. So we reworked it, this time asking our best friend to put it together for us. The new profile book was more personal and I think it showed more of our personalities. We gave it to the agency and, again, we waited.

Then came the near-misses, the times when our caseworker called and said something about staying in touch or a birthmother being interested. We got our hopes up, only to have them come crashing quickly down to earth when "the call" never came. And every group meeting, we continued to hear the numbers: the number of birthmothers, the number of families. We calculated the odds and still no call came. One year turned into two and we became pretty discouraged. I was silently glad we hadn't set up the nursery yet and we stopped making purchases for the baby. It got even harder to go to the group meetings and we started to skip some.

At that point we began to consider some alternatives. We talked to our Indiana agency and learned they were starting to do actual placement work, rather than just pre- and post-placement work. Their approach was more modern, though, with more responsibility placed on the families for some of the marketing legwork. We thought about it and decided to put our hat in their ring as well. Now we had two agencies working for us and all it cost Novia and I was a few thousand dollars for the Internet and marketing training. So we started that process as well. We took the online courses, worked on our social media profile page and waited some more.

Then it happened: We got a call! A birthmother about six weeks from her due date had chosen us. The caseworker gave us the details: She was a young African-American woman, not yet twenty and pregnant with a seemingly healthy baby boy. However, the problem was that this birthmother was considered "high risk" for disruption, meaning the agency wasn't really confident that she would place the baby. We had heard these stories before and knew it could be heartbreaking, but what were we going to do? Turn down the match? We'd waited so long and had no idea when or *if* another birthmother might choose us, so we forged ahead and accepted the match.

We met with the birthmother, talked about our plans, answered her questions and just tried to make sure we didn't say or do anything that might cause her to change her mind and pick another couple. We began the whirlwind of preparations for welcoming a newborn: painting and decorating his room, putting the furniture and equipment together, buying more supplies and clothes and diapers. We got everything ready. We even went to one of the birthmother's doctor appointments with her.

Then we met with our attorney and learned about the various hoops we'd have to jump through for both Novia and I to become the child's legal parents. We knew through my earlier research that Indiana was one of the few states that allowed second parent adoption, meaning a person not married to the biological or legal parent could adopt the child without that legal parent giving up their parental rights. In essence, it meant gay couples could both be legal parents, which was not the case in most states. But it also meant I had to legally adopt the child first. Kentucky did not allow gay couples to adopt, so in their eyes, I was the only one adopting him. After I adopted him, Novia would then have to file a separate petition to legally adopt him in Indiana as his second parent. Two separate adoption actions and two sets of adoption expenses! But we were prepared to do whatever was necessary to make sure our family was legally protected. So again, we pressed on.

As the due date drew near, we grew increasingly excited and anxious: excited to welcome our son into the world, yet anxious about whether the birthmother might change her mind. We made plans to take an extended leave from work following the birth and arranged for family to help take care of our house and pets while we stayed in the hotel with the baby for what could be weeks. The due date came and the social worker told us they were scheduling an induction for the following week if the baby hadn't arrived by then. When the induction date came, the social worker called again. This time she told us not to come to the hospital; the birthmother wanted to wait until she was discharged before we could come get the child.

The red flags couldn't be ignored any longer. We knew it was a bad sign and that she was likely to change her mind. In the end, that's just what she did. After the baby was born, the birthmother decided she wanted to parent the baby herself. We got another call, the one that all prospective adoptive parents dread, telling us she had changed her mind and that we wouldn't be taking him home with us after all. To say we were devastated doesn't adequately convey the loss and grief we felt. We both left work immediately and went to a restaurant to talk and try to digest what had just happened. It was a very, very difficult experience. But we also knew we weren't ready to throw in the towel and give up on our dream of having a family, so we told the agency to keep us on the active list.

More months passed and we were now the oldest family in the agency, the couple that had been waiting longer than all the others. We'd watched family after family come and go. Some came back again for child number two while we still waited. We revamped our profile book one more time after seeking some feedback. I did this one myself and made it even more personal, displaying what I thought was our fun personalities and lifestyles.

Going on our third year, we got a call one day from our caseworker in late April 2012, almost exactly one year after our first matching call. She told us we needed to get our paperwork updated: It had to be kept current every year and we were a little behind in the update. She came right out and told us, even though she wasn't supposed to, that we had to do it immediately, because they had a birthmother who was due "very soon." The birthmother had decided she didn't want to choose the parents for her baby and would let the agency do it. This happened on occasion and when it did, the agency would match the child to the family who had been waiting the longest. That was us! But they couldn't match us if our paperwork wasn't current, so we scrambled for several days to get it done.

The caseworker wouldn't tell us anything more about the situation for privacy reasons. We didn't know what "very soon" meant, so we had no idea when we might expect "the call." We anxiously waited and tried very, very hard not to get our hopes up too high. A week went by, then another, then another. We finally decided that something must have happened and the birthmother had changed her mind, either about placing her baby or about choosing the parents. This was probably just another near miss. So again, we went on living our lives and waiting.

On Monday, May 20th, I stayed home from work, because I wasn't feeling well. I slept in and once I got up, I was lounging around the house in my pajamas. My cell phone was still on vibrate mode from work (we have no home phone, just cell phones). A little after 11:00 A.M., I happened to check it and saw five missed calls and numerous text messages from Novia. I immediately called her back and she told me to call our caseworker. After she couldn't reach me, our caseworker had eventually called Novia but couldn't tell her anything, because, according to Kentucky, I was technically the adoptive parent. She did, however, tell Novia that I would want to take this call!

To say my heart was racing would be the grossest of gross under-statements. I think it raced so fast it stopped while I made that call. My hands were shaking so badly I "fat-fingered" the numbers on my cell phone and had to erase them and redial. When our caseworker answered, she said the words I had hoped to hear for more than three years:

"We have a baby for you!"

I think she tried to give me all the details, like the baby's race and health status, but I didn't care. We had a baby! I know she asked if we wanted to adopt him and I'm pretty sure I screamed "Yes!" into the phone. She told us to come to the hospital and pick up *our son*. I don't think I breathed again for about an hour. I called Novia right back and somehow I passed on the information to her, although I think I mostly just said, "Come home!"

Novia came right home and we threw together some things we'd need for an overnight stay at the hospital, called a friend to come take care of our pets and then rushed to the car. We had already packed what we called our "deployment" bag (military backgrounds!) and it had every-thing we thought the baby would need for the first several days, since we knew we couldn't take him across state lines for a while. We'd also left the baby seat installed in the car from the year before when we were matched. We were pretty much ready to go, so we threw the deployment bag in the trunk and off we went.

We made a quick stop on the way to pick up some things for the birthmother and a few gifts for the nurses and arrived at the hospital by 2:00 P.M. I'm not sure our hearts ever stopped racing, but they were certainly racing again as we approached the hospital room. The birth-mother's social worker met us and started bringing us up to speed. I honestly don't recall much about that conversation, except that she told us it was a healthy baby boy, the birthmother was twenty years old and African-American, the birthfather was Caucasian and not in the picture and, most importantly, she had chosen us as the parents. I remember asking if this was the birthmother who had not wanted to choose the parents for her child and she told me it wasn't. This was a "surprise" birthmother, meaning she hadn't even contacted the agency until she gave birth, so they rushed right over with some potential parents' profiles and she had picked ours!

One other thing I do specifically remember about that conversation was the story the social worker told us about how the birthmother had picked us. The social worker had given her our profile book first (we were the longest waiting family, after all) and the birthmother immediately connected to the cover photo, which was a picture of us swimming with dolphins. Apparently she loved animals.

As she turned the pages, she found photos of us skiing and snowboarding. She loved snowboarding, too. When she saw the snowboarding pictures, the social worker said she pulled the book to her chest, hugged it and told her this was the couple she wanted. The social worker told her to take her time and look at the other profiles, but the birthmother said no, it was us! My heart just stopped with that story and I knew right then that this little boy was meant to be our son.

The next day was easily the most emotionally difficult I've ever experienced, as we met with the birthmother, got to know her a little bit, answered her questions and held our breath, hoping she wouldn't change her mind. She clearly loved this child and was making this decision for no other reason than love, wanting him to have the kind of life she knew she couldn't give him at that time. It was obvious this was a very difficult decision for her. She allowed us to hold him right away and feed him. After a short time, the birthmother went into her room to rest. The nurses let us stay in the room next to hers and she left him with us while she napped.

I went out and picked up some dinner for everyone and after the birthmother rested, we visited with her again for a little while. Her only request was that she wanted to have the baby in her room with her for the night and said she would bring him to us in the morning. So we lay down on our hospital bed and tried to sleep, tried not to worry, hoped against hope that she wouldn't change her mind and *waited some more*.

About 5:00 A.M. the next morning, the birthmother lightly knocked on our door and came in with the baby. We talked about how his night had been and how she had slept. Then we took some pictures for her (that I immediately printed on the portable printer I had brought with us for just this purpose) and started the painful process of her saying goodbye. We promised her that we would give him the best life we could and would always make sure he knew how much she loved him. Then we all cried while she said goodbye. (I still cry to this day every time I remember those moments!) She placed him in my arms, kissed him and walked out of the hospital room and out of his life.

Even though this was an open adoption, the birthmother had told us that other than the agreed-upon photos and letters from us telling her how he's doing for a few years, she didn't want any future contact. I think she knew it would be too hard on her. She did give us her e-mail address and we knew her full name, but we had not given her our last names, out of an overabundance of caution. Part of her story involved an overbearing parent who didn't know about the baby yet, so we were concerned that if he found out, he might pressure her to come back for the child later on. But after meeting her, we also knew that once it was legally "safe" to do so, we would be okay with her being a part of his life in some way if that's what she wanted. She was certainly a very loving, intelligent, thoughtful and beautiful young woman and we will be forever indebted to her for entrusting us with this most precious gift.

We left the hospital later that day with our little five-pound bundle of joy and headed to the hotel. Over the next two weeks, we took care of little Christopher James, kept in touch with our attorney and the two adoption agencies and dotted every "i" and crossed every "t" they told us to. After two weeks, we got the go-ahead from the state of Kentucky to take him home, across the state line to Indiana, while we waited (again) on the rest of the adoption process to play out. Finally, an eternal three months later on August 22nd, we met with an Indiana judge.

I finalized the adoption and just moments later, Novia was able to finalize her Indiana second-parent adoption. Unfortunately, the law in Kentucky didn't allow same-sex couples to be on a birth certificate together, even though Novia was still legally Christopher's parent. Regardless, the finalization was a glorious event for us. The judge signed two adoption decrees, we took some pictures and finally, all the waiting was over! Christopher was now a forever part of our family.

# Matthew Smith and Trey Darnell

JOHNSON CITY, TENNESSEE

Hello! We are Matthew and Trey from Johnson City, Tennessee. We are the second-most famous Matt-and-Trey combo in the United States. First place belongs to Matt Stone and Trey Parker, the creators of *South Park* and *The Book of Mormon*. Our spot in second place status is secured just ahead of the Matt-and-Trey serving team at one of our local dining establishments.

Matt was born in Glendora, California and is employed as a registered nurse. I am a native of Kingsport, Tennessee and flying high as a commercial airline captain. Our story as a same-sex couple began in 2007 through the power of social media. A connection sparked over a picture of Matthew standing in front of a fast food restaurant. Matthew and I are best friends. We are very competitive with each other and laugh a lot.

In August 2012, while on a road trip to Charlotte, North Carolina, Matthew and I decided to take our relationship from "two is company" to "three is a crowd." We already had the usual criteria before starting a family: solid careers, a large enough home, a big yard and financial stability. So there we were, staying at an inn in Charlotte, when we looked at each other and said, "Let's adopt!"

When someone wants to learn more about a specific topic, what do they do? Look it up online! We did our due diligence that night in researching the process of adopting, possible agencies and the differences in open and closed adoptions. Matthew and I decided to pursue an adoption over a surrogacy to prevent the dilemma of which one of us would be the biological father. We are indecisive when trying to decide where to have dinner; we could only imagine the process of deciding who would be the sperm donor. E-mails and information requests allowed the excitement to build. At this point, it was way past midnight and we needed sleep before our return home the next morning.

While still feeling the euphoria of all the positive information we had obtained from our online research, we didn't just float back to Earth; we came crashing down. Matthew and I soon received the following e-mail from a prominent domestic adoption agency:

> Mr. Darnell,
>
> Thanks for asking about our Domestic Program...Our agency has not proved to be the best fit for same-sex couples as the birthparents looking to make an adoption plan for their child through [the agency] are overwhelmingly looking for more traditional married couples to place with. That tends to be the reason they come to our agency...I certainly do not wish to mislead you or "just take your money" when the chances of receiving a placement would be unlikely.

A traditional married couple? There was no way we would ever fit into that category. Our state did not recognize marriages, civil unions or domestic partnerships of same-sex couples at that time. Questions of doubt started to form. What were people going to think and say? The e-mail was not meant to be hurtful, but it was successful in being destructive.

Now what? How does one go from a pessimistic view to a very optimistic attitude? Go on vacation! So we took a weekend trip to Atlanta, Georgia, to attend a free informational session offered by a large adoption agency. We were both surprised to learn that it was also the same weekend of Atlanta Gay Pride. I personally had never been to a gay pride event before. Did you know the group Dykes on Bikes always starts a gay pride parade? I can honestly say that weekend with the agency and the events changed everything for us.

As a same-sex couple, Matthew and I had the unique opportunity to share our story of growing a family through adoption. Instead of marketing ourselves as a couple hoping to adopt, we were given a platform to promote gay couples parenting in general. There has never been a greater moment than now for us to open up about our lives. As each day passes, equal rights for LGBT individuals are growing. Now is the time for us to share and to speak. When we started the adoption process, it was our hope to expand our family with a child and now we are able to help spread the positive message of gay parenting.

When we wrote the first draft of our profile letter, it was twice as long as our agency recommended. It is very difficult to condense everything you want to say into fewer than one thousand words. Our adoption profile was approved for viewing by expecting parents the week before Christmas in 2012. At that particular time, the average waiting period for a same-sex couple was fifteen months, though we were both well aware that our wait could end up being shorter or much longer than that.

Matthew and I had decided to promote ourselves as a couple in every way possible for six months and then take a step back and evaluate our approach. Over the next couple of weeks, we had a few contacts from potential birthmothers. All of them we considered to be emotional scams. Every waiting family is aware of the risks that adoption can bring. In most cases, families get angry with these particular situations, but we chose to use them as practice experiences to get over the nerves of talking to pregnant women.

In March 2013, we received a text message on our designated adoption cell phone number. We were both just coincidentally looking at the phone when the text was received. It said, "How do you feel about twins?" We were stunned, giddy and nervous. We had always been open to the idea of twins. Over the next couple of weeks, we talked to this particular expecting mother and all three of us seemed to hit it off very well. There were so many similarities: She was a registered nurse in Labor and Delivery and liked most of the same things we did. We had several phone conversations with her and learned that she had contacted our adoption agency and that she was also speaking to another family as well. Matthew and I both felt like this was the right match for us.

This birthmother was very cautious about the adoption process and had several specific concerns. She was mostly terrified that once the adoption occurred, the adoptive parents and her twin girls would disappear. There was only one state, California, in which open adoption agreements were considered legally enforceable. In all other states, they were primarily promises.

While talking to the mother of the twins, we missed another incoming text message. Since we didn't respond to the text within a couple of hours, we then received a call on the toll-free telephone number that was listed on our adoption profile. When someone dialed the number, Matthew and I received simultaneous calls on our personal cell phones, as well as the house phone. Needless to say, when all three phones rang at the same time, we started to panic.

This phone call was from the mother of an expecting father in Texas. She asked many questions and I felt an instant connection with her. We had come to a crossroad. Matthew and I liked both situations. The twins were due in June and the Texas baby was due in September. We decided to continue with both possibilities for the time being.

Over the next several days, we knew the Texas situation was moving fast and would probably result in a match very soon. We presented both situations to our adoption coordinator and asked for advice. It became apparent that we needed to disclose the Texas situation to the mother of the twins.

It was a very hard and emotional conversation. The mother of the twins was devastated. At that point, she was still determining whether she would parent or place her twin girls. She wanted us to parent if she chose not to, but she said it would break her heart to prevent us from matching with this other expecting couple. She insisted she would not stand in the way of us becoming dads. It was very difficult to end this potential situation, but when we received an e-mail including a sonogram photo from Mercy and Dylan, the expecting parents in Texas, we knew this was our perfect match. Mercy mentioned in the e-mail that the baby looked like a T-Rex.

Matthew and I matched with Mercy and Dylan on April 10, 2013. I still have the voicemail saved on my phone. Mercy had just entered her second trimester at that time, so we fit into the category of a long match. This meant we had the opportunity to be present for a majority of the pregnancy and build a strong foundation for our relationship that would last a lifetime.

A few weeks after we matched, it was time to determine the sex of baby T-Rex. Matthew was working the day we were supposed to find out, so I purchased two balloons: one pink and one blue. Then I waited outside of the hospital where Matthew was working. The next sixty minutes seemed to take hours. Finally, Mercy sent a wonderful text message that caught me completely off guard:

It's a girl. YAY!

I grabbed the pink balloon, quickly entered the hospital and got in the elevator. As I exited the elevator and looked to the left, I saw Matthew working on the computer at the nurses' station. I had the pink balloon hidden behind my back. Before he had time to say anything, I presented the balloon to him. We were able to enjoy that moment together after it had unfolded over one thousand miles away.

Soon the time came for us to travel west and meet Mercy and Dylan in person. Near the end of May, we said goodbye to our cats and flew out to Texas. Our flight arrived in Dallas and then we rented a car to make the three-hour drive to the town of Abilene.

Matthew and I dealt with a lot of stress leading up to that meeting. It seemed to escalate while driving to Abilene. We were overly excited and nervous to meet the expecting mother and father for the first time. The moments leading up to the meeting felt like a first date after building a foundation of communication with them over the past month.

A counselor from our agency was there to facilitate the match meeting. He had reserved the children's activity room at a library for everyone to get together, but there was not much about this exceptionally large space that indicated either children or activity. It was full of six-foot tables and chairs and did not have that small, quaint feeling we had hoped for. Matthew and I picked a table in the middle of the room and allowed our anticipation and nerves to grow even more.

Before long, we heard a library representative tell someone, "The activity room is located in the back." Mercy and Dylan were here. I'm pretty sure Matthew and I both stopped breathing. As the expecting mother and father seated themselves across from us, Matthew quickly stated what I think everyone was feeling: "I know we are all extremely nervous." With that, the ice had been broken. Questions were then posed to both couples and with each answer the meeting seemed to get more and more comfortable.

Thirty minutes quickly turned into an hour and a half. During that time, we learned about Mercy and Dylan both as individuals and as a couple. Looking back on the match meeting, all of the stress left as we said goodbye to the counselor and began our weekend in Abilene with Mercy and Dylan. I'm thankful for those anxieties, though, as they allowed us to be aware of this truly memorable moment and made us more prepared for the spectacular time that was in our near future.

Over the next few days, Matthew and I were welcomed into an energetic, funny and loving family. We were able to spend time with parents, grandparents, siblings and cousins. Each and every one of them made an extra effort to show their support for us as a couple and the potential adoptive parents of their future daughter, granddaughter, great-granddaughter, niece and cousin. We listened to stories and told a few of our own. A couple of the stories were somewhat embarrassing, but we learned about Mercy and Dylan's family and they learned about us. There was a lot of laughter all around. Some family members commuted from hours away and everyone made sure they had ample time off from work to meet and support Mercy, Dylan, Matthew and me. We felt so welcomed and loved by this family and were extremely excited to merge them with ours.

The final night was marked by an epic family barbeque—Texas style, complete with cloth napkins, table decorations and a metal T-Rex sculpture. The menu included brisket, baby back ribs, sausage and jalapeño peppers stuffed with cream cheese, wrapped in bacon and then grilled to perfection. The evening was certainly a celebration, a family celebration that Matthew and I were a part of. There was not a better way to end our visit to Abilene than by enjoying each other's company after a terrific Texas family BBQ.

I have to admit it was a little emotional saying goodbye to everyone that night. Over the past three days, it felt like we were already a part of their family. But luckily, Matthew and I knew that this goodbye was only for a short period of time: In just a few months, Baby T-Rex would make her arrival. We were extremely excited about what the future held for our entire family, which had now grown much larger.

As the summer quickly started to fade, we knew it could be weeks or merely days before we had to make the 1,128-mile trip back to Abilene for the birth of Baby T-Rex. When you're on "baby time," there are no easy planning or travel solutions. Blogs, books, lists, parenting forums and workshops do not prepare you for getting a phone call saying the expecting mom is at the hospital with contractions and you are over a thousand miles away.

As we entered the last five weeks of pregnancy, Matthew and I worked through several available options to get us to the hospital as quickly as possible. We had tentative travel plans to arrive in Abilene a week before the due date. But what if the baby decided to make her appearance sooner? There was an alternative plan in place for that: One of us would be on the first available flight and the other would drive. We also made arrangements for our cats, mowing the lawn and anything else we could think of. The goal was to have everything packed and ready to go at a moment's notice by mid-August.

It was the second Thursday in August when we received the news that Mercy's labor could be imminent. I hate to admit it, but Matthew and I were definitely caught off guard. It seemed as if clothing, baby clothes, diapers, cameras and cats were flying in every direction. The car was packed full with what felt like half our house and a car seat was securely in place. Everything happened extremely fast. Anxiety and excitement took complete control.

On this particular Thursday, travel by air wasn't an option, so Matthew and I both buckled in and began the seventeen-hour drive to Texas. We received numerous text updates from Mercy's family through-out the evening. The miles were slowly ticking off. I swore the odometer was not working correctly. Our late night turned into early morning and there had been no change in Mercy's condition. When we reached Memphis, Tennessee, we decided to stop and get some much-needed sleep.

As the sun rose on a hot and humid Friday morning in west Tennessee, we learned that Mercy's imminent labor was a false alarm. The expecting mother had a stalled labor and was now receiving medication to stop the contractions. Everyone was grateful that she was resting comfortably. Matthew and I took a deep breath, smiled and buckled in for our trip back home.

After arriving in Johnson City and unpacking the car, we began creating a staging area in our guest bedroom for everything we wanted to take with us on the real trip. Bags and containers were unpacked and repacked more efficiently. The false alarm had been a practice drill that we were able to learn from. Without question, it was an exhausting twenty-four hours, but we made sure that we were better prepared for the next call. *Now* Matthew and I were ready to leave at any given moment.

Monday, August 19, 2013, started just like any other day. It was business as usual and we were still anxiously awaiting the arrival of Baby T-Rex. Only ten days had passed since our false-alarm trip across the state of Tennessee. Travel plans were being finalized and time away from work had been scheduled. Only twenty-three days until the due date. Then everything completely changed with four text messages:

Dilated 6

We are on our way to labor and delivery

We are having baby tonight

Wahoo

Reading those four messages created feelings of anxiety, excitement and stress. The baby was coming *tonight*? Seriously? My first phone call was to Matthew while he was still at work. When he answered, I could only muster up a three-word phrase: "Leave work now!"

The next hour included packing clothes, stacking up bags and crates in the car, checking on available flights to Texas, calling our parents and waiting for Matthew to make the thirty-minute drive home from work. We had already experienced our practice drill, so we were prepared to leave as quickly as possible. All in all, it took ninety minutes from the phone call to when we pulled out of the driveway. As the garage door was closing, I thought to myself, *The next time it opens, we'll have our daughter with us and be a family of three.*

Matthew and I had barely driven fifty miles before we were hit with the reality of just how long it was going to take to get to Texas. The GPS indicated that we still had seventeen hours to go. In the past, we had talked about listening to an audiobook together, so what better time to try one than now? A quick stop at a bookstore in Knoxville, Tennessee, and I was already over the idea. I hadn't even heard of half the books available. One of the few titles we recognized was *The Help*, so forty-nine dollars later and we were back on the road. By Disc 1, Track 3, I was already lost and had no idea what was happening in the story. We had seen the movie while it was still playing in theaters and yet I couldn't even keep up with someone reading the story to me. This was going to be a long trip.

The miles seemed to pass slowly and the chapters of the book even slower. We both regularly checked our phones for updates from the labor and delivery floor at the hospital. The current plan was to induce Mercy at 8:00 A.M. the next morning. Our GPS indicated that if we continued to drive through the night, we would arrive at 9:15 A.M. Everything appeared to be happening in our favor. Then we received a text message saying that the medical staff had broken Mercy's water. *What?* We had just driven through Nashville, Tennessee, and still had hundreds of miles to go.

Less than two hours later, as we were speeding toward the Tennessee state line, we received two more text messages:

Hopefully she won't have to push for long

Liz says she is done

The baby was here? We were dads! Matthew and I needed a moment to process this, so we took the next available exit off I-40 in Jackson, Tennessee, to fill the car up with gasoline and grab a quick bite to eat.

As I was sitting down with my food, my phone vibrated with another text message. This time it was a small image. It had to be a picture of our daughter. I held off looking at the picture until Matthew seated himself next to me in the booth. We clicked the image and it grew bigger. *There she was!* The very first picture of our daughter. Reminiscing about that moment still gets me a little choked up: two guys, same side of the booth, looking at a phone and getting very emotional at a fast food restaurant in Jackson, Tennessee. It was definitely a head turner.

After discarding the half-eaten fast food, we hopped back in the car and continued to process everything that was happening. Matthew drove around to the back of the building and that's when the tears began to flow. Our world had just changed forever. It was very tough to let that reality sink in. There was definitely some sadness about missing her birth, but we were still happy and very excited. It was hard to believe the baby was finally here. We really wanted to be at the hospital with Mercy and Dylan, but were elated that both mother and baby were doing fine.

Before pulling back onto the interstate, we got all of the information that any parent should be able to rattle off to a random stranger. Harper Wade Darnell was born August 19, 2013, at 8:24 P.M. She weighed 5 pounds, 9.6 ounces and was 18.5 inches long. Harper was given my last name. Her middle name is the last name of one of Matthew's great grandmothers.

Exhaustion had set in. It was well past midnight by the time we crossed into Arkansas. My excitement—or lack thereof—for *The Help* had not changed. I found myself constantly checking the CD info display. Disc 5, Track 13. *Sigh*...We were barely able to keep our eyes open, so we chose to stop for a brief nap and a refreshing shower.

Our alarm went off at 6:00 A.M. the next morning and it was time to start the day. Excitement and nerves were overpowering: We were anxious to meet our new baby girl. We had five hundred miles left to go and I immediately wondered if Matthew had forgotten about *The Help*. No such luck! Disc 6.

Arkadelphia, Texarkana, Dallas...Abilene! Eight hours later, we could see the hospital. We had finally arrived. I have to admit we were very worried about what we would encounter during the hospital stay. Matthew and I had heard about the unpredictable hospital adventures of other families adopting a newborn. Some had great experiences, but some had horrible ones. A same-sex couple adopting in Texas did not sound too positive. As the elevator doors slowly opened with the sound of metal rubbing against metal, we had no idea what to expect. The hospital episode had started.

Walking down the hall to Mercy's room, we were greeted by many of the nursing staff. They were eager to give us the armbands that allowed unrestricted access to our baby and tried to contain their excitement while asking about our drive. I refrained from mentioning *The Help*. One of the nurses finally apologized and stated that we probably wanted to meet the little girl. We did! As we quickly continued on toward Mercy's room, Dylan's mom appeared in the hallway. Her smile immediately put us at ease.

We walked into the room and saw Mercy sitting on the bed holding the smallest human being I had ever seen—sweet little Harper. We quickly hugged Mercy and everyone else in the room before we laid our eyes on the new baby for the first time. It is hard to describe the emotion of that moment.

As the next several hours passed, we had the chance to feed, diaper, cuddle and kiss our little girl. Mercy had been cleared for discharge that afternoon, but Harper had to stay through the night so the medical team could monitor her body temperature. The hospital gave Matthew and I our own room so we could spend our first night together with Harper as a new family. Mercy was ready to be discharged, but she requested some time alone with the baby first. With all the constant visitors, she hadn't gotten any mother-daughter time with Harper. Everything had been moving in a positive direction until the nursing shift changed. In fewer than ten minutes, it all quickly turned to chaos.

The night-shift nurse entered the room and insisted she needed Harper's car seat that instant. A few minutes later, the baby was wheeled out of the hospital room for a two-hour car seat test. It didn't take long for our protective instincts to kick in. Matthew chased the nurse down the hall to explain the circumstances. We pleaded with her, asking to delay the car seat check until later that night, so Mercy could spend some time with Harper before leaving. No luck. Emotions had reached the breaking point. The lack of sleep accompanied by the magnitude of the adoption plan was not the best combination. In the end, Mercy was discharged without having what she really needed: alone time with her baby.

In light of what happened with the night-shift nurse, Mercy decided to get some rest at home and planned to visit the next day. We offered her our room when she did. She was our main concern at that moment: It was our goal to make sure that Mercy had everything she wanted or needed at the hospital. To give her some extra space while visiting with Harper, Matthew and I decided to get some fresh air and grab something to eat.

When we got back to the hospital, we received the good news that Miss Harper was being discharged. We let Mercy pick an outfit for Harper to wear on her way out. Mercy carefully evaluated all of the options and made her selection. Then we, as Harper's posse, walked out of the hospital with bags, blankets, pillows, diapers, formula and a car seat. The nurse made sure that Harper was buckled securely into her car seat. We hugged everyone and made plans to have dinner later that evening.

When we arrived at our hotel, the staff was waiting patiently for us. Before we even opened the car door, many staff members were peeking out from the lobby. Everyone was hoping for a quick glimpse of the new arrival.

As we opened the door to our room, we were met with another pleasant surprise. The entire hotel staff had signed a banner that exclaimed: "It's a Girl!" They had also filled the room with pink balloons and pink flowers. We were in awe of their amazing hospitality. It felt like Texas had rolled out the red carpet and welcomed us with open arms.

This was our first real night alone with Harper and the first chance to settle into our new roles as parents. However, like others who have adopted or are in the process of adopting, Matthew and I were just theoretically babysitting until the relinquishment documents had been signed and the revocation period was completed. For an agency adoption, there is no revocation period in Texas and the relinquishment documents cannot be signed until forty-eight hours after the birth of the child. Our counselor was traveling to Abilene from Houston and had scheduled a meeting to sign all of these documents at three o'clock the next afternoon. We began holding our breath. Our nerves were out of control.

Matthew and I had already planned to stay in Abilene through the weekend and leave on Tuesday morning. It is not uncommon for an adoptive family to leave town immediately after the relinquishment documents are signed, but we chose to wait an extra five days. We wanted to spend as much time as possible with Mercy and Dylan and the rest of the birth-family. Matthew and I wanted to reassure everyone that this was not a goodbye: It was a new beginning. We were very committed to the idea of an open adoption.

Thursday, August 22, 2013. The day had arrived that could truly make us dads. The hotel graciously offered a vacant suite for our counselor to use. Mercy and Dylan's mother, Stacie, came to the hotel a few hours before the meeting. While Stacie and I talked about everything from food to medical insurance, Matthew got carried away with the digital camera. It seemed like every couple of seconds the sound of the camera shutter echoed through the room. The results were phenomenal. We still look at those pictures often.

Soon our adoption counselor from the agency arrived and asked who wanted to go first. My heart started to beat faster. I felt nauseous. I couldn't think straight and every possible outcome played out in my head.

Everything was happening very fast. After what seemed like only four or five blinks of an eye, she returned and asked Matthew and I to sign two forms. We were now officially dads!

The counselor posed for a couple of pictures, asked if we had any questions, gave everyone a hug and then left. I held my composure as plans were being made with Mercy and Stacie for later that night. Everyone gave hugs and said a quick goodbye, as we would all be back together in just a couple of hours. When the door to our room closed, Matthew started to do his quirky happy dance. We hugged each other, hugged Harper and then one of us asked, "Now what?"

What would any person in the trenches of the social media world want to do after a moment as monumental as this? I quickly typed a status update on my profile and added a picture. But before I pressed the "post" button, we began to worry about Mercy. While Matthew and I were overjoyed, we wanted to be respectful of Mercy and the rest of the family. We agreed to at least tell our parents they were officially grandparents and gave them permission to share the good news with the family, but not online.

As the afternoon quickly faded away, we headed out to spend the evening with the birthfamily. It is hard to describe the feeling of being a new parent. Matthew and I were on cloud nine. We wanted to ask permission to share the news with our friends and family on social media. Matthew mentioned our concerns about making a post to our online profiles and Mercy and the family said they were somewhat disappointed we hadn't shared the news already. A world record then occurred for the fastest status update ever.

Over the next several days, we spent as much time as possible with Mercy, Dylan and the rest of the family. We watched the MTV Music Awards together. How could we miss *NSYNC's reunion in honor of Harper's birth? I think I squealed (inside) five or six times during the ninety-second performance. An indication of a good match is having similar tastes in music.

The weekend ended quickly and we were less than twenty-four hours from leaving Abilene. We had scheduled Harper's one-week appointment for that morning with the pediatrician who had administered care in the hospital and we invited Mercy to join us. Later that evening, Mercy, Dylan and Dylan's sister-in-law, Liz, invited us to their home and cooked a wonderful southern meal. During dinner, I could feel the emotions rise to the surface. The excitement of starting our journey home and the sadness of saying goodbye to Mercy and Dylan were at their all-time highest. Abilene had started to feel comfortable. As the night came to an end, we made plans for our final goodbye the next day.

Mercy arrived at our hotel a couple of hours prior to checkout. Our plan for the first leg of our trip home was to drive three hours to Dallas and spend a couple of days there. Then we were going to slowly make our way to the Texas-Arkansas border while we waited for approval from both the Texas and Tennessee Interstate Compact for Placement of Children (ICPC). Mercy and Harper were able to have some alone time while Matthew and I loaded the car. Over the past week, we had undoubtedly acquired more stuff, so now the car barely had any room left for us. Before the trip was over, we had to return a few things due to the lack of available space.

As checkout time came and went, we began to say goodbye. Matthew and I wanted to reassure Mercy that we would be back soon. This was the beginning of a new journey for all of us. We inched a little closer to the door. All three of us hugged, with Harper sandwiched in the middle. Tears were flowing as we said the last of at least fifteen goodbyes. Mercy slowly walked to the elevator, our room door closed and Matthew and I fell apart. We were delighted to leave Abilene, but we also felt as if we had just broken the heart of our child's mother. That was a moment I will never forget.

It is very possible that we sobbed for fifteen minutes while leaning up against that door. In my mind, it felt like the all-too-common scene from the movies where two people are crying on either side of a door and neither one of them knows what's happening on the other side. We managed to compose ourselves and snuck out of the hotel, hoping the staff wouldn't see us leave. The car was loaded to the brink and we were ready to go.

At that point, we had been in Texas for a week and were beyond ready to be home. Our family was anxious and impatient. It was absolutely exhausting not knowing how long it might take to get approval to leave Texas and then having two full days of driving after that. Add a newborn into the mix and you just want to hit fast forward. Feedings were approximately two to two-and-a-half hours apart and lasted almost forty-five minutes each. We were lucky to make it an hour and a half driving at any given time.

While on the road, we started to get stressed since we still had not received approval to leave the state of Texas with Harper. As our luck would have it, it was the start of a holiday weekend. If we didn't get approval that day, we would be stuck in Texas for at least another four days. Tensions ran high.

The call we had been waiting for came just twenty miles from the state line. Our adoption counselor told us that we had just received ICPC approval. So long, Texas! We were Tennessee bound.

As the miles slowly added up, we were getting closer and closer to home. We began to contemplate how to introduce Harper to her grandparents. Allowing them to come to our house was quickly ruled out: We love them dearly, but once they got there, they might never leave. Giving each set of grandparents the opportunity to meet Harper and have their special moment with her was important. We didn't have the heart to be only a few miles away and say, "We'll see you tomorrow." So we came up with one stipulation, just one tiny rule: We would visit with them now, but only for one hour each. Then each set of parents would have the opportunity to see all of us again, hopefully refreshed, the next day.

With a little resistance, they agreed, and two-and-a-half hours later we found ourselves in the car again on our way home, where our cats and recorded television shows were waiting. It was our house that hoarded all of our stuff, stuff that we had definitely missed. It is hard to believe that you can miss stuff. Is it weird to hug a toaster?

Finally, the road trip was over. Our journey to become parents was complete. Life as dads had just begun.

- *Twelve days*
- *2,581 miles*
- *Five different hotels*
- *One audiobook*

Over the next several days, Matthew and I started to settle into the routine of being at home with Harper. We were amazed at the instant popularity we received by having a newborn. Looking back on that time, I remember constantly being asked if we were tired. Being tired had nothing to do with the newborn and everything to do with the family visitation that came from being new parents.

It was only two weeks into Harper's life when we were dealt a heavy blow. Harper was a little jaundiced, so we had been treating her with a bilirubin blanket at home for several days. We scheduled a pediatrician appointment for her on a Friday and were hoping to get the good news that we could stop using the bilirubin blanket. But the day didn't proceed as planned.

Harper had been undergoing daily blood tests for the past week. Over a three-day period, her hemoglobin had dropped to a critically low level, requiring her to have a blood transfusion. Harper didn't have the chance to complete the intake at the hospital before the doctor ordered her to be transported by ambulance to the Pediatric Intensive Care Unit (PICU) at the children's hospital a half hour away.

Matthew and I were emotional wrecks. We were scared, confused and speechless. Inquiries were made about the medical history of the birthfamily. We were asked question after question. One of the positive aspects of an open adoption is having access to the health records of the birthparents and birthgrandparents. In one of my obsessive moments, I had scanned all of this medical information and had it readily available on our smartphones.

Harper was moved to a private room where many doctors and residents surrounded her. Then she was quickly taken away to receive an IV. My parents had met us at the first hospital and travelled with us to the children's hospital, but now Matthew and I had reached the point where we needed some alone time. My parents gave us a hug and reluctantly left.

Within a few moments, Harper was returned to the room. She had an IV inserted into her head and bandages were stuck to both arms where attempts at starting an IV had failed. As the staff exited the room, Matthew and I fell apart. Even to this day, seeing Harper like that is the toughest thing that I have ever experienced.

Before we had a chance to process everything that was happening, Matthew's parents arrived at the hospital. Matthew's half-sister began to tear up when she saw Harper with all of the tubing and cords that monitored her vitals. We politely asked Matthew's family to leave and allow us to support each other and Harper. It was definitely an emotional moment for everyone involved.

There was one positive outcome of this intimidating experience: It really helped to solidify our new family unit. It was one of the first times in our lives that Matthew and I had to turn to each other for support and not rely on our parents for comfort in this moment of uncertainty. It was now time to claim our position as the parents and be strong for our daughter. Over the next four days, we continued to stand strong for our new family.

On the first night in the PICU, Harper stayed under two enormous blue lights for the jaundice. Her red blood cells were breaking down at an alarming rate and the cause was still unknown. Her body was not producing red blood cells fast enough to replenish the blood her body required. She needed a blood transfusion while the physicians worked to determine the cause. Until all of the tests were completed, Harper was not allowed to eat.

One of the most difficult things in life has to be caring for a sick infant. Harper was so hungry and crying for food and there was no possible way to explain to her what was happening. The bilirubin lights required her to be blindfolded. She was connected to several different monitors and a pump administering her blood transfusion. We were unable to pick her up and hold her. The only method of comfort came in the form of a small glucose solution, which provided a few drops of sugar and water to calm her when she cried of hunger.

Harper underwent a heel stick every couple of hours over a four-day period to monitor her hemoglobin levels. In the end, she only needed one transfusion. Harper is currently six months old and under the care of a hospital hematologist. We still do not have an explanation for the rapid destruction of her red blood cells, but her body is now producing enough of them to maintain what is considered a normal level. The hematologist continues to monitor her condition and will conduct an extensive round of testing within the next month. Harper provides every indication that she is a happy and healthy little girl.

When going through the adoption process, your desires and path to become parents is very open and public. There is really no privacy during the process, so Matthew and I decided to make our wedding private. Since same-sex marriage was not legal in Tennessee at that time, we had to travel to one of the states that allowed us to enter into holy matrimony.

We planned a four-day trip to Washington, DC, for just the three of us. The first day included applying for a marriage license and the last day saw a beautiful ceremony in the Botanical Gardens adjacent to the United States Capital Building. The in-between involved a lot of walking, paintings, stuffed animals and First Lady dresses. This was our chance to do something very private and memorable as a new family of three. There were no worries about a cake, which side of the aisle guests would sit on or a first dance.

At this very moment, I am sitting here with two cats and a giggling baby staring at me as I put our story into words that will outlast our vivid memory. I can tell you that Matthew and I feel ecstatic about our journey to parenthood. We are also proud to declare that we are a same-sex couple from East Tennessee and exceptional dads. We have the same desires as any parents and those include providing a loving and safe home for our daughter—well, that and cute baby clothes.

We are less than twenty-four hours away from finalizing our adoption of Harper. In the morning, Matthew and I will appear before a judge in Washington County, Tennessee, who is going to make us her legal parents. This is the last step of the adoption process.

Tennessee does not currently have legislation that makes it either legal or illegal for a same-sex couple to adopt a child. In our situation, we have a very forward-thinking attorney who has built solid relationships with various judges in the region. These judges look at each individual case and focus on how the new family is working together mechanically and what is best for the child. There is no focus on the gender of the parents.

While tomorrow morning will bring a conclusion to this eighteen-month-long process, there is still one minor detail to complete: Who gets to be listed as Harper's mother on the Texas birth certificate? Texas has yet to update the outdated birth certificate format which hasn't changed in decades. A few states have replaced the title of Mother and Father with Parent A and Parent B or something of that nature. Some of our friends who are going through the adoption process have struggled with this decision, but for some reason, Matthew and I find this to be a fun little memento that one of us will get to have.

Having completed a successful adoption together, we are typically asked one general question about our journey: How long did it take until you became dads? From the day we decided to start the process until the day Harper was born, it took just 366 days.

Looking back over the past year and a half, we have definitely experienced a lifetime of happiness and disappointments. We have laughed and cried. Our emotions have mimicked a thrill ride at an amusement park. Now that everything is all said and done, we are dads, both legally and emotionally. No one can change that now.

When the process first started, we were worried about being at a disadvantage because we were gay. That worrying carried over into wondering if we were too young or not looking the part of typical parents. Would we even relate with expecting parents?

The process of adoption is full of uncertainties, hope and heartache. Adoption is also not for the faint of heart. But one thing is definitely true: When you become a mother, a father, Parent A or Parent B, it is worth the bumpy road it takes to get there.

# Manuel and Dale

CLOVIS, CALIFORNIA

We were having trouble getting this started, so we decided to begin with our son's bedtime story. We talk to him about his adoption as openly as possible. He didn't really understand the concept until he started pre-school. Now he is all about, "Some kids have a mommy and a daddy, some have one mommy or one daddy, some have two mommies and some have two daddies like me!" We chose the open adoption route to have communication with his birthmother and, in time, with him about the process.

We want our son to be okay with sharing or not sharing his story. Ultimately, it will be his choice. We've learned that strangers feel it's okay to make random comments like "He must look like his mom" or "He could pass for your son." At first we didn't know how to respond, but now we just hold our heads high and say, "Yes." We've learned through the years that our response will shape his responses.

For now, this is our journey, starting with our son's first bedtime story, which shaped itself during his first year and was inspired by a cosmic night light that still shines in his room:

Once upon a time, there was a very Special Star in the universe that was looking for the perfect parents. He asked his birth mommy to help him find the perfect family and she said, "Yes."

One day she picked up the phone and called Daddy and Papa to see if they wanted to meet her. Two days later, the very Special Star came down, down, down from the universe to tell his birth mommy that these were the dads for him. The Special Star flew back into the universe, waiting for the perfect time to come back down. A week later, the Special Star became impatient and came down again to test out his chosen daddies. So Daddy and Papa got in the car and drove up, up, up, hoping to meet their very Special Star, but it wasn't time yet. Daddy and Papa stayed with birth mommy in the hospital to make sure she was okay and had everything she needed before coming back home to wait.

Halloween came and no Kyan. Then Thanksgiving came and still no Kyan. Daddy and Papa had finally decided to just wait for their Christmas baby when the call came. Our very Special Star started to come down, down, down from the universe at 3:00 A.M. So Daddy and Papa got in the car and drove up, up, up to meet their very Special Star from the universe. Daddy and Papa got to the hospital at 5:00 A.M. and were able to be with birth mommy during this most magical time. Our Special Star was flying around making sure everyone was okay and then you were born at 8:05 A.M.

Once you saw that birth mommy was okay, your Daddy and Papa were okay and you felt in your heart that you would be okay, you sent your very Special Star back into the universe to help your brother or sister find their way home, too.

During the years of waiting, we had several false alarms. We started off as a potential foster family, hoping to turn a placement into an adoption. We had two prospective matches with our agency and were extremely excited for each one; however, our hopes were crushed when both matches fell through. Both times we prepared a room for our potential "instant family," but the children were placed in different homes. This left us with a horribly empty feeling, having to face the completed rooms day in and day out.

When we finally got over those losses, we rallied one more time and began to research adoption. We came across a nearby agency on the Internet and became familiar with the open adoption process. We later found out that one of our friends was already using the same agency and this helped us decide to go with them.

After being added to the pool of potential parents, we were put in contact with a local birthmother who decided she wanted to place her child with us. We had talked to her via a contact who made it seem like everything was on track. However, we later discovered that the match had gone sour when the birthmother's extended family did not want the child raised by two dads. They stepped up at the eleventh hour and made promises to help the young mother of two. After numerous phone calls and a resounding agreement to place her child with us, she finally backed out on New Year's Eve, 2009. We had such high hopes, investing so much time and emotion, only to have everything fall apart at the last minute. We were heartbroken.

Our family was all set to come over and help us ring in the New Year. The potential match had been so strong that we had already made plans to announce it to both of our families that evening. The birthmother was so sure that she was going to place with us "no matter what," but it didn't work out. Instead, we had to put on brave faces and make sure everyone was tended to before the New Year struck. It was such a hollow New Year's Eve, but we said, "We still have each other. Everything will happen when the time is right."

Each time a match fell through, we thought we wouldn't be able to go through it again. Although our agency cautioned us to remain openhearted but detached of emotion, it became difficult when we got caught up in the moment. We just couldn't stop our hearts from loving and wanting, but we had to.

Our agency offered support group meetings for parents-to-be and this was a time when we really needed them. Although the closest meeting to us was a three-hour drive, we managed to make it when we could. Once we got there, we quickly made friends with other prospective parents. We had a chance to hear their stories about matches falling through and felt okay about our own situation. It was important, at that time, to realize that matching and un-matching was pretty common. Some couples were taking calls and turning people away. Others had received no calls at all and weren't shy about asking for referrals.

We just sat and listened and took it all in. Road trip discussions have always been the best way for us to talk things out as a couple and determine our next step in life. On our way home, we were able to do exactly that and we decided it was best for us just to wait. We always believed our child was out there in the universe, circling around, looking for us.

So we waited and networked, talked to others and held our breath. Then one day we finally got a call from our agency about a potential match. Our parameters were a bit wider than most, so we received calls about possible matches with birthmothers who had mental health issues, some drug or alcohol use and other special circumstances. This call was pertaining to a birthmother who thought she was due any day. We arranged to meet her two days later at our agency's home office. The adoption counselor made introductions and then left us alone to talk. After a few minutes of small talk, we all realized that we had a lot in common and really felt comfortable with each other. We laughed at similar experiences and cried at some revealing moments, but in the end, we felt good about the meeting.

We were able to cut to the chase about placement and why we were selected, at which time the birthmother suddenly exclaimed: "You are the ones for this baby!" We soon discovered that was her style—call it like you see it. We didn't judge her lifestyle or really question her reasons for wanting to place her child. We were just there, hoping that she saw something in us that clicked—and she did. By the end of our four-hour meeting with the birthmother, we all felt that we were on the right track for the best possible solution to her situation. We were officially matched on October 22, 2010.

We had very little information about the birthfather except for what our birthmother told us. She explained that their interaction was brief and intense. She provided a name and large city where he reportedly resided and described his age, race and physical attributes. She indicated to us that she had contacted him shortly after confirming her pregnancy, but he had denied the baby was his. The birthfather issue was one which we chose not to push—we could sense whenever it was discussed that our birthmother wasn't too keen about going into details beyond what she had provided.

A week after our match meeting, our birthmother thought she was in labor. We made all the necessary arrangements for our pets, home and work and began the three-hour drive up to the hospital. Halfway there, our birthmother called to let us know it had been a false alarm. We asked if we could still come up anyway, which she agreed to. When we walked into her room, we heard the baby's heart beating. It was music to our ears.

Once our birthmother announced that we were the dads and gave the doctors permission to talk to us about her condition, we learned that the baby was healthy, just not ready yet. They couldn't determine an actual due date at that time. Arrangements were made for our birthmother to visit a prenatal clinic and an imaging center in the next few days. Once we made sure everything else was in order and that our birthmother was being taken care of, we left for the drive home.

Our birthmother invited us to attend any of her appointments if we wanted to and we did. We had waited a long time to become dads and wanted to experience as much as possible. The first ultrasound provided us with a clear image of our future baby and also determined that it was a boy. It was very exciting and we felt so fortunate to have been a part of that moment. Around that time, we also learned the baby was due in late November or early December. Our birthmother found a clinic that was able to give her late-evening appointments so we could be there with her. Every Wednesday, we road-tripped up north to pick her up and accompany her to the clinic. She was never shy around us and never minced words with anyone about who we were. She always declared, "They are the dads!" End of story.

The doctors we met at the clinic were very good, but the nursing staff on those special Wednesdays were truly amazing. They made us all feel at ease, letting us know what to expect and when to expect it and always hoping to "See you next Wednesday." All of this time was really important for us to get to know our birthmother and for her to get to know us and our little quirks.

Prior to our last clinic visit, we decided to have dinner together at a local pizza place. Our birthmother had heard of one of their house specials called the "Prego Pizza." It was heavy on the onions and garlic and believed to induce labor. Nothing happened that night except good food, good company and good memories. Over dinner, we revisited the fact that we hadn't been the first family picked, but we all felt we were the perfect match for each other. We left that dinner feeling good about life, our connection to the birthmother and the real possibility that we were going to be daddies soon.

After the first false alarm, we had our bags packed and ready to go at the drop of a hat. By now we knew we were having a boy, so we had all of his things prepared as well—including a car seat. Two days after the Prego Pizza, our birthmother went into labor.

She called us at 3:00 A.M. "I'm headed to the hospital."

We said, "We love you and we'll see you soon." We were up and out the door in fifteen minutes. We drove to the hospital in record time. When we arrived, the reality hit us that the next time we walked out of that hospital, we might very well be dads. Every moment was emotional and surreal. When we finally walked into our birthmother's room, it was 5:00 A.M. She was happy to see us, but not really in a talkative mood. Suddenly, we realized that we didn't really know how to help. That was where our labor and delivery angel came in, Nurse Christy. She was just amazing! She had actually read our birth plan and put us right to work.

She said, "Daddy, stand here. Papa, stand here and assist Mom in whatever she needs. Don't panic and be ready." She fluttered about us from 5:00 A.M. to 8:00 A.M., including us in everything she was doing. After one final check, she declared, "It's time." Nurse Christy called in the doctor, took us by the arms and said, "This is it!"

Our son was born at 8:05 A.M. and in that moment of time, our whole world changed. Our hearts pounded, adrenaline rushed through our veins and huge grins appeared on both of our faces. We were finally dads.

About thirty minutes after he was born, another nurse brought the birth certificate paperwork into the room where it sat staring at us for approximately an hour. At some point, we could sense our birthmother's anxiety about it, so we asked her if she wanted our help in completing it, which she did. We read off each line and she responded to the questions. We had previously discussed with our birthmother that we wanted to name the baby Kyan and give him our last name. We were very lucky that she was open to this, because we didn't have to change his name when we updated the birth certificate to reflect us as his parents.

Almost six months to the day after his birth, a good friend who happened to be a Superior Court Judge finalized Kyan's adoption. The judge had received special permission to transfer our adoption into her court and finalized the legal process on our behalf. Despite being told to expect the birth certificate several months later, we were quite surprised to receive it within three weeks instead. Something about seeing the three of us on the birth certificate created a sense of security and "wholeness."

We had heard so many horror stories from various people about how adoptions had fallen prey to myriad factions of demise. We had been warned by our adoption agency from the minute we opened the door for orientation about all of the "what ifs" and "what to do when things don't go the way you planned." We had mentally prepared for many of the potential pitfalls and attempted to stay two to three steps ahead of the process at any given time, knowing that the adoption could go off the rails at any moment. Seeing the birth certificate with our names in proverbial dry ink provided an intense and deep sense of reassurance, the magnitude of which we had never experienced before and haven't since.

We remain in regular contact with Kyan's birthmother. Once in a while, we'll get a text or a phone call from her. We send pictures and leave the door open for a face-to-face meeting whenever she is ready. We also remain in contact with the amazing nursing staff at the prenatal clinic and our labor and delivery nurse, Christy. We send them pictures and keep in touch via e-mail. I'm sure at some point there will be a time when Kyan will want information about his birthfather. Other than the description his birthmother gave us, we still really don't know anything else about him. This will be new territory for all of us, but we plan to advocate on his behalf when that time comes.

When Kyan turned one year old, we decided to go through the process all over again. We really want our family to grow and for our son to have a brother or sister. Peppered with sage advice about the "dos and don'ts" of parenthood, our families continue to support our decision to become dads. Our son has brought so much joy into our lives and we only hope that we have provided our birthmother with the peace of mind that her birth child is happy, safe and thriving. We owe her so much and are eternally grateful to her for allowing us to be present and for bringing such a beautiful child into our lives.

# PART 2

# FOSTER PARENTING AND ADOPTING FROM FOSTER CARE

Foster care is a situation where minors are temporarily placed into safe environments in the event that they are unable to live safely with their families for some reason. Children could end up in foster care as a result of neglect, abuse, divorce, the death of a legal guardian or a plethora of other unfortunate events that could disrupt a home. If you choose to become a foster parent, you will play a major role in adding stability to a child's life by providing a safe home environment in his or her time of need. Foster care is designed to be a temporary solution until a child can be reunited with his or her previous parents or guardians, meaning you will only be caring for the child during a short transition period. However, reunification is not always possible and sometimes this temporary care can lead to a more permanent situation through adoption.

As with open adoption, foster care comes with its own unique rewards and challenges. You won't have the hefty fees associated with surrogacy or private adoption and you may even receive a monthly stipend to help feed, clothe and meet the basic needs of the children placed in your care. While money should never be a reason to become a foster parent, it does help with taking care of a child. You will also have numerous resources to guide you along the way. Still, caseworkers are often overworked and prospective foster parents sometimes endure long wait times as a result.

Also, while not always the case, foster children may come from homes that were broken by drugs, sexual or physical abuse, financial hardship or many other scenarios. Because of this, there is a possibility that they may have developed aggressive behavior or emotional insecurities that could disrupt your household. There are also many children in foster care with medical issues, developmental delays and/or physical disabilities. Support is available to help you adjust, but it is important to fully understand a child's background and how your life will be impacted before you decide to open your home.

When you foster a child, you also may have interactions with a child's birthparents that may not always be positive. Keep in mind that even if you work with an LGBT-friendly agency, the child's birthparents or family members may not be so accepting. They might even be openly antagonistic toward their child growing up with gay or lesbian parents.

Finally, when you open your home to a foster child who has nowhere else to go, you're not only helping them, but you're helping their family and community as well. This is particularly true for LGBT youth. Unfortunately, there are still kids who get kicked out of their homes because of their sexual orientation or gender identity. It can be hard for LGBT children in foster care to find permanent homes. It can also be hard to find people willing to take in a child with HIV/AIDS. As a prospective LGBT parent, you are in a unique position to help kids in our community grow up in a safe, stable and accepting environment.

For those of you interested in becoming foster parents, this section details the diverse experiences that some same-sex couples have had when raising children from the foster care system. What is it like to care for a child who came from a broken home? Is it difficult for same-sex couples to get approved as foster parents? What does it feel like to bond with a child, only to have them leave your home shortly thereafter? Each story in this section provides a different perspective on the challenges and rewards of foster parenting and adopting from foster care.

# Cori Ferguson and Casey Garrison

ST. LOUIS, MISSOURI

Casey and I decided to have kids after we had been together for several years. We were both married before to men, but didn't have any children from those relationships. Casey has an auto-immune disease which made getting pregnant nearly impossible for her—stopping all of her treatments as needed could have had disastrous consequences—so we decided that I would be the one to have a baby.

Initially, we tried to do things at home with the help of our very good friend acting as a donor. At that point in our lives, our insurance did not cover infertility and we couldn't afford the cost of paying it all out of pocket. We tried to get pregnant for several years using this method with no success. We were blessed that our good friend was so patient and committed to put up with it for that long!

We finally came to the conclusion that we needed some help, so I went to my OB/GYN. She prescribed medication that stimulates ovulation and referred us to another doctor who did artificial inseminations. My OB/GYN was fully aware that Casey and I were in a same-sex relationship, so it surprised us when her referral was for someone in that same office, because it was part of a Catholic university hospital.

We met with the doctor. He offered us his help, but said the only people in his office who could know were his nurse and the billing person. He swore them both to secrecy, because if the administration found out, the doctor could lose his job. We were astounded to learn that he was only going to charge us $250 each time!

So we began the journey. Each month I used ovulation tests for about a ten-day period. When we got a positive, we headed to the doctor's office the next morning, after meeting our donor friend on the corner of our street to get the sample. Casey tucked the specimen cup inside her bra to keep it at body temperature and also to hide it when we got to the doctor's office. It was really quite comical. We used to joke that the neighbors were going to think we were buying drugs and imagined everyone's surprise when the cops discovered our secret hand-off was actually sperm!

After that, it was a waiting game for a week or so until I took a pregnancy test. Following the second round with the doctor in June 2011, one pregnancy test came back positive. We were ecstatic! Years of disappointments melted away when we saw the results. Sadly, I miscarried seven weeks into the pregnancy. It was probably the single darkest moment of our lives. Casey and I each grieved in our own way and finally came to the conclusion that maybe we were meant to go in another direction.

We started to investigate the possibility of adoption, but private adoption can be very costly and the process can take a long time. We discussed whether we might consider adopting a child from foster care. Was it even possible for us to do that as a same-sex couple living in the very conservative state of Missouri?

Missouri's Department of Children's Services stated that they didn't discriminate based on sexual orientation, so we decided to go for it. But since Missouri didn't allow second-parent adoptions if the parents weren't married, we also decided that I was going to be the one listed as the licensed foster parent—my income was higher and we felt they might look at that as more stability. We submitted my application, making sure to include Casey in the answers so it was very obvious and clear that this was a joint effort.

The city of St. Louis was fantastic. They treated us no differently from anyone else and it gave us hope that this choice was going to work. They allowed Casey to attend all the same courses with me for free so she also could be educated as a foster parent. The second set of classes we attended was in a different county, so we were apprehensive. It was the country people, not the city people, who were less accustomed to diversity. Thankfully, everyone in the class treated us respectfully, even though there were many couples who made it clear that they were very religious.

While we were going through the sixty-four hours of required training, the home study and the background checks, our St. Louis caseworker occasionally sent us profiles of children who fit into the categories that we were willing to consider. We had gone into this expecting to end up with a three- to five-year-old child, because we were seeking adoption only and not fostering. On a Friday morning in May 2012, our caseworker sent us the profile of a ten-month-old African-American boy. She told us that she needed to know by the following Monday morning if we were interested in him, because they wanted to move forward with placing him in a pre-adoptive home.

Casey and I read that profile dozens of times over the weekend. We talked to our best friends about it and Casey talked to her mom, who is a registered nurse. The profile indicated that the baby had some significant developmental delays. At ten months old, he wasn't sitting up or crawling yet. They also said he couldn't eat regular food, so he was still on baby food and formula. The family history had indicated his birthmother was borderline mentally challenged and a history of developmental disabilities existed in his extended family.

We finally came to a decision together that it was better for us to have a baby who might have some delays and medical issues than an older child with behavioral and mental problems due to abuse. So we said "Yes, we are interested!" Honestly, I don't think either one of us thought we had a chance of having him placed with us, because babies out of foster care are rare and we had the perceived handicap of being a same-sex couple.

A month passed and, just as we were about to give up, the caseworker called and told us that we were one of three couples selected to be interviewed for him. We were shocked and nervous. We had less than a week to prepare ourselves for what we jokingly called the Spanish Inquisition.

On June 25th, Casey and I went before the care team, which consisted of caseworkers, supervisors and the current foster parent. The interview lasted about forty-five minutes. We did our best to read what they were thinking, but still left there feeling completely stressed out!

They told us to expect an answer by the next day. We decided to go to one of the local casinos after the interview to get our minds on something else. As we were sitting playing video poker, my cell phone rang. It was our caseworker with a few more questions the care team wanted us to answer. We were encouraged, because it was 6:00 P.M. and they were still deliberating. Clearly we were still in the running if they wanted to ask some follow-up questions.

About thirty minutes later, my cell phone rang a second time. It was the caseworker again. This time she asked if there was somewhere we could go to put the phone on speaker: She wanted to talk to both of us at once. We made a mad dash to the quietest place we could find, which was the women's bathroom. There were people inside, but we didn't care. The caseworker said, "I just wanted to know what color you are going to paint Xavier's room."

Once Casey and I both caught on, we started jumping up and down, hugging each other and screaming, "I can't believe it! They picked us!" I'm sure the other women in the bathroom were staring, wondering what in the world was going on. For that moment, we were the happiest people in the world and nothing else mattered.

We had been told the agency wanted to move quickly with the baby's transition from the foster home to ours and they weren't kidding! We had less than a month to prepare for our lives and home to change drastically. We emptied out our spare bedroom and repainted it. We needed to buy everything a baby needs, including a crib, high chair, car seats, clothes and more. We also had to schedule time off from work to bond with him when he came home. All the things you normally have nine months to prepare for, we had four weeks!

We met Xavier for the first time two weeks after being selected. We visited him in his foster home. He had been in the foster care system since he was three months old and we weren't sure what to expect, given the information we had read in his profile. We hadn't even seen a picture of him at that point, but Casey and I knew this little boy was our son.

Casey sat down on the floor where Xavier was scooting around on his belly and he immediately pulled himself over to her lap. We had been told he didn't really display any emotion, didn't smile and was scared of crowds. We talked to him, played with him and then we saw a ray of hope. The oldest daughter of the foster family came home and when she walked into the room, Xavier's face lit up with a huge smile.

During our second visit with Xavier, I was feeding him baby food when he started to gag—the caseworker told us he threw up all the time when he ate and that he had problems with chewing and swallowing. This time when Xavier gagged, I quickly blew into his face. It startled him and made him forget all about gagging—so no throwing up! He thought it was funny and started to smile at us. We knew by the end of that first week that this child had potential; he just needed attention and to be loved.

On July 21, 2012, one week before his first birthday, Xavier came to live with us permanently. Oddly, Xavier was born the week before we lost our baby in 2011. It was something we felt was more than a coincidence: He was meant to be our son.

And so it began. Our journey has been loaded with some fantastic people who have openly accepted our relationship. In fact, everyone we've worked with, from Xavier's caseworkers to his therapists (he has physical, occupational and speech therapy) has showered us with compliments and said we are exactly what Xavier needed. Xavier has blossomed from that baby who couldn't sit up and was afraid of crowds to a very smart two-and-a-half-year-old who runs, talks and shows affection. He just needed someone to believe in him.

Xavier's adoption was finalized on October 24, 2013. We decided to keep his first name the same, because we love it. His middle name is now Cory (after me) and his last name is Garrison (Casey's last name). We also had the opportunity to meet Xavier's birthmother and his baby sister (Xavier is one of seven siblings) before she voluntarily signed away her rights. The birthmother requested to meet us before she did. She was very thankful and felt comfortable enough to ask whether we might consider taking Xavier's baby sister too if she ever came into the foster care system. Casey and I assured her that we would absolutely take her into our home.

Our message to other LGBT couples is to believe! If you want to be a parent, believe it will happen for you. It may not be the way you planned it, but be open to other avenues. You may be surprised how many supportive, accepting people you find on your journey, like doctors, nurses, caseworkers and judges. The world is changing and you can't live in fear. Be proud of who you are and don't be afraid to go after what you want!

# Duke and Steve Nelson

### DALLAS, TEXAS

I always knew I was meant to be a dad. I remember thinking about the kind of parent I wanted to be: the kind who cuts the crusts off peanut butter and jelly sandwiches and helps make rocket ships out of building blocks. I wanted to help my kids with homework and projects. I wanted to take them to parks and museums.

When I was a kid, we didn't have much money. But my sisters and I had a really good childhood—not idyllic or perfect, but happy. We went camping in the snow, took road trips across the country and hit up every roadside attraction from coast to coast. With all those adventures came the stories, stories that defined and helped me become the person I am today. Growing up, I always imagined myself having a family as well—I also envisioned becoming an architect and marrying a red-headed woman. Boy, was I way off. So for years, I pushed those things aside.

But the dream of a family was always with me. It was the image of being a dad and having kids who I could share my own experiences with and create new ones. I wanted to be at little league games and dance recitals. I wanted to sit around the dinner table and share stories of when my mom was a little girl. I wanted to kiss boo-boos and sneak money under pillows after the excitement of losing a tooth. Being an uncle is great, but it's not the same as being a dad.

When I met Steve, we were nineteen and thought we had it all figured out: Be together forever and have a family. Easier said than done. The trouble was there weren't many role models out there to show us that we could have kids, much less how to do it. Life has changed quite a bit in the past twenty years.

There was very little mainstream gay—no *Will and Grace,* Ellen and Rosie didn't have shows yet, Neil Patrick Harris was still Doogie and Lance Bass was still on tour with *NSYNC. We didn't know any same-sex couples who had kids. We knew they existed, but like the Loch Ness Monster, they were the things of legend.

I guess this is the reason I want to share our story, to help others who want the same and don't see their reflection in their own families or communities. I want them to learn from our mistakes, to exist and be visible, so we can all just be dads and not "gay" dads.

Many years and many ups and downs later, Steve and I were gearing up to celebrate our fortieth birthdays and agreed that if we didn't do something soon, our own personal window for fatherhood was going to close. Over the years, I had researched adoption and surrogacy. We had friends who had gone both routes and we grilled them, learning more with every conversation, article, book or website. Each time we thought we were ready to make a decision, we weren't. Work, life, our relationship—anything became a perceived obstacle or an excuse.

One night we were in bed talking and doing some research on adoption in our home state of Texas. That's when we came across the TARE website, through the Department of Family and Protective Services. The website showed so many kids—all ages, races and personalities—with these bright faces and amazing smiles, desperate to find a family and home where they could be safe and grow, where someone could take care of them and let them realize their potential. That did it. We signed up for a foster care class the next day. We were extremely focused. Five weeks later, we got approved by the state for foster care and adoption. That was quite a process.

The first foster care class reminded me of college English 101—a bunch of people there on the first day, which eventually dwindled down to four or five by day three. In an effort to share the "reality" of being a foster care parent, the instructors actually made it a bit scary. But we were not going to be deterred.

Throughout the whole process, we were never treated differently because we were gay. We did a little research, so the agency we selected was accepting of LGBT foster parents. In fact, we were even asked to come back several times to speak to new groups of foster parents, both gay and straight, about our experience.

We moved through the training faster than they could schedule it. We had to stay on top of everything from scheduling to paperwork, just to make sure there were no delays. Getting the city to come and approve our house took the longest. We had to schedule that ten days in advance.

The training sessions were mainly concerning safety—quite a bit of common sense with a splash of technique. It seemed the largest focus was on liability. It was all good information, just not exactly what new parents might need. Apart from not harming the kids, there was absolutely nothing practical—like which formula to buy or how to change a diaper. For that, we had to use our network of family and friends.

The other foster parents in class were divided into two camps. One group was like us: people looking to adopt or to contribute to the community through the temporary care of needy children. You could tell who was in this group by the questions they asked. Some of them even had kids in their family who were already in the custody of Child Protective Services (CPS) and they wanted to care for them specifically. The other group treated foster parenting a bit more like a business with a clear return on investment. We heard personal stories of kids stacked ten deep in foster houses and parents getting certified to accept even more. It is a desperately needed side of the foster care system that we had no idea existed.

Home visits were interesting. They looked for random things. We were asked to move our eggs to the bottom shelf of the refrigerator. Because we were fairly informed of the state's standards, we actually discovered discrepancies between the state and agency we used. We learned early on to ask lots of questions—sometimes more than once.

The day we got our license, three children were placed in our home. It was crazy. I got an e-mail one Friday at noon with our license and a follow-up phone call stating our names had been put in the system to accept any race, sibling group of up to three kids or any child aged under six years old. At three o'clock, I got a phone call letting us know we were picked for an emergency placement. The only information I had was an e-mail with three bios that had the wrong races and genders on them.

Steve was flying home from a work trip, so when he landed he had a bigger shock. I at least had a couple of hours to adjust to having kids. Steve only had about thirty minutes and a handful of text messages.

At five o'clock, the kids were dropped off: all under three years old, all related and all in diapers. There was Sean, a month shy of his third birthday and our little escape artist, who could unlock the front door and tried to work the microwave in the first twelve hours. Next came Luc, who at eighteen months showed no emotions except when hungry, not even responding to his own name. And last, but not least, was Willow, beautiful at six weeks old, who slept on my chest for the first two weeks.

We were in love. Overwhelmed, but in love. That love got us through the first few weeks of the dramatic change in our lives. At one point, we even considered backing out, because we were afraid of getting so attached and then possibly losing them. It was the most emotionally difficult time in my entire life.

By the third week, Steve and I had decided that no matter what happened, whether the kids were with us for a month or for the rest of our lives, we were going to give them everything we could. Steve later told me about the moment he realized that Luc could be his son: Steve was eating something in front of the TV and Luc walked up, looked at the plate and smiled at him. Steve gave him a bite.

My moment came at the end of the first two weeks. I was exhausted and surviving on minutes of sleep at a time. Just when I thought I couldn't get out of bed or mix another bottle or change another diaper, I watched Willow sleeping on my chest. She was so quiet, so peaceful. I knew at that moment that I would do anything for these three beautiful children.

While we took care of the kids for the first nine months, they had weekly visits with their birthparents. Early on, the birthparents were at every visit. That fell off as time progressed. When we first heard the mother's backstory, we were really rallying behind her. From what the caseworker shared, she had been dealt a pretty rough hand and it looked like the fathers were at least making an attempt.

Then we met them.

The mother spent more time on her phone than she did with the kids. We wondered why the kids never asked about their mom. During the visits, they didn't even acknowledge her presence. It was like she was someone they knew, but weren't excited to see—almost as if they didn't recognize her. It was really strange. Both fathers were in and out of jail, one a registered sex offender. There were no questions from them about the kids, like how they were doing or what they were eating. The birth-parents didn't make eye contact at all during the visits.

It wasn't until their parental rights were terminated that we saw each other eye to eye. Even though we were on their side in the beginning, they viewed us as a couple of guys who were trying to take away their kids—like CPS—so our interactions were not always positive. We understood their apprehension.

CPS's process is focused mainly around reunification. We knew that going in. When the kids first came to us, CPS was already vetting fourteen different family members who could potentially care for them. That took almost nine months. Each family member was removed from the running for one reason or another: some only wanted one child, while others had a criminal record or a record with CPS. The children were not going to be placed back with their parents, but it became very obvious that there were no viable candidates within the family. In Dallas County, there is a goal to have a plan for the kids by the six-month mark. By month nine, CPS informed us that they planned to split up Sean, Luc and Willow and try to place them with some of the fourteen original family members who did not pass CPS's initial review.

We were shocked and heartbroken for the children. They had known no other existence than with each other. The thought of them trying to adjust not only to a new environment, but a new environment without anyone they knew, was terrifying.

We discovered that, in Dallas County, foster parents typically have no rights regarding the future of the children unless they've been placed in care for more than twelve months. We were not only some of the first foster parents to argue for a place at the table prior to twelve months and win, but we were also the first same-sex couple that we know of to do so.

At the end of the nine-month mark, parental rights were voluntarily terminated and we petitioned to adopt the kids. The adoption process took another nine months. We had no other hurdles, but there was always the worry or fear that someone might come out of the woodwork and lay claim to one or all three of the children.

It took us one day shy of eighteen months for everything to be finalized—and we are still working on finishing Steve's legal adoption today. Since I was the parent licensed—at the time, Texas didn't offer joint licensing for same-sex couples—I was the primary parent. Steve and I are getting married this year and he's changing his name. At that point, we'll complete his adoption of our kids.

It was a long road and at times we thought we might lose the kids or our minds. We are very lucky and very happy. There are many things they don't tell you about foster care and adoption. I didn't realize how much bureaucracy and red tape comes with a government agency. It was a forty-hour workweek just managing the paperwork, visits and appointments, added onto a full-time job and chasing two mobile toddlers around. To this day, I still haven't figured out how I gained weight during the experience.

We had committed to the birthparents to allow monthly visits with the kids. We've never heard from one of the dads and the other parents were no-shows so often that we opted out of continuing the visits. After talking with the kids' doctor, it seemed the best approach was to end all contact at that point.

Fast forward to now. We are a bit like the "It's a Small World" ride at Disneyland: Steve is Hispanic, I'm Caucasian and our three kids are African-American. When we pile out of the car, we know we all look so different, but it hasn't really mattered. We take each of our cultures and heritages seriously, but not so seriously that we can't function.

It does mean that we get quite a bit of attention. Most of it is positive and accepting. We have been pleasantly surprised at how accepting people are when they realize that we are a family. Rarely, there is a look of confusion; even more rarely, a look of disgust or anger.

When you put information like wanting kids out into the world, the world always gives you lots of information back, usually in the form of advice. Most of the advice we've gotten has been spot on—even if it was unsolicited and, at the time, sometimes unwanted.

Family and friends with kids are always quick to share their experiences—some good, mostly bad. You hear the sound of doom in their voices:

"Your life won't be your own."

"You'll never sleep again."

"You've got to pick the right school."

"Hover versus don't hover."

"Stay at home versus day care."

There are opposing views on almost everything when it comes to kids. Who knew parenting could be such a competition?

Steve and I thought we knew what to expect from this advice. Boy, were we wrong. Well, except for the comments about never sleeping again. That part is true. Between listening for tiny whimpers or coughs in the night and worrying about their overall happiness and well-being, I don't think Steve and I have slept a full eight hours between the two of us.

But it's more than that. Everyone tells you about that stuff, but no one tells you why you worry, why you sneak into their room and watch them sleep or why you try to protect them from everything. It's because these kids change you; they change you completely, right down to your cells. Everything you thought you knew about yourself becomes different. Advice doesn't prepare you for the experience.

No one could ever prepare me for the rush of feelings I get when I hear "Daddy!" after walking through the door. No description can do justice to the feeling I get on a cold Sunday morning when two of them sneak into bed and snuggle. No words can describe the fear and worry when a little runny nose turns into a hacking cough and we debate if this warrants a trip to the emergency room or not.

The future has more in store. Will Sean do well in school? Will Luc make friends? Will Willow meet someone special (please, please, please after she's twenty-one)? I worry about them sneaking out with their friends, buckling under peer pressure and getting hurt on the soccer field or whatever sport they may or may not choose to play. I worry about them being good and kind people and loyal friends. I worry about the choices they make every day.

Nope, no one can prepare you for why you feel this way. There's no brochure at the adoption agency, online video or class you can take. It just happens. And you are caught off guard, completely immersed.

It's been a wild ride. I can't believe it's been over two years since those three came into our lives. We've already started having our own amazing adventures.

# Diana Buchbinder

SAN FRANCISCO, CALIFORNIA

A lot can change in thirty years and this is especially true where gay parenting is concerned. When I started this journey in 1981, most gays and lesbians who were parents had conceived their children as part of heterosexual relationships. During that time, the time of Anita Bryant, the Briggs initiative and the beginnings of the AIDS crisis, coming out as gay meant risking everything, including your job and your children. At the age of twenty-eight, I fell in love with a woman, divorced my husband and came out. Of all the possible repercussions associated with that decision, the only one I was truly concerned about was how it might affect my ability to become a mother.

My husband and I did not have children together, although I loved children and taught at a preschool. I had always intended to have some of my own one day and my new partner assured me that I still could as a lesbian. But I was unsure how to proceed. The idea of gays conceiving and being allowed to adopt was still very new and not widely spoken of. There was not yet a network of fertility clinics, although there was a small underground circle of community women who served as "go betweens" for women who wanted to conceive and men who were willing to be sperm donors.

Adopting as a lesbian was pretty much out of the question, as social services did not consider single people desirable parents—straight or gay—and most placements offered were hard-to-place kids, either because of age or social/emotional/medical issues. The political tenor of the times made it risky for social services to place children with gays for fear of the press if something went wrong. The gay community was fighting for acceptance on many fronts at that time and parenting seemed like either a frivolous or unattainable goal to some. It was not uncommon to hear lesbians attribute their political activism to being free of the burden of child-rearing. Gay men, along with fearing for their lives due to the AIDS crisis, were weighed down by the sorrow of believing that fatherhood was irretrievably lost to them, because of whom they loved and how they were perceived.

I decided to take two different approaches to achieve parenthood and pursued both adoption/foster care and conception at the same time. I saw a flyer from our local social service agency looking for mental health professionals to participate in an experimental program creating therapeutic foster homes. The goal of the program was to place school-age children with social/emotional issues in a foster home environment, rather than in residential treatment. I applied and was accepted into the program along with my partner. In the group with us were three straight couples, two single women, one gay man and one gay male couple. We underwent an intensive ten-week training period, as well as certifications, background checks and home inspections. At the end of our training, we were each assigned a foster child. A seven-year-old girl was placed in my home.

Unfortunately, the girl eventually moved to a residential treatment program after all. But the impact of her coming to live with us and then being taken away was profound. It made my partner and I realize that we were unprepared to deal with a child who had severe psychological trauma without significant resources. We didn't know how to find those resources, how to ask for them or how to navigate the social service system well enough to get her and ourselves the support we needed. Although we understood she had needs that were beyond what we could provide, her move to residential treatment made us feel like failures, even more so when the agency advised us to sever all future contact with her, because it might have interfered with her ability to adjust to the new location. We were devastated. In time, we did wind up reconnecting and are currently in contact with her on social media.

Although the child placed with us wound up moving to residential treatment and the program was not sustainable beyond a couple of years, bonds were created among the group. My partner and I became very close to the gay male couple and together we made plans for me to conceive a biological child that we could all parent together. Co-parent relationships were legally untested and we went to great lengths to be precise about our expectations and responsibilities, reducing everything to writing.

We decided to have the two men act as donors and mix each sample to increase inclusion. Unfortunately, conception was more difficult and took longer than we expected. In the end, our parenting plan did not survive the stress and disappointment of several miscarriages.

After the therapeutic foster home experiment, my partner and I decided to apply for the fost/adopt program through social services, hoping for the placement of an infant that we could ultimately adopt. Although social services did accept our application, we could not apply as a couple, so only I applied and I was considered the potential fost/ adopt parent. When we asked for assurances that my application was going to be considered equally with all the others, we were told that there was no written policy as to how gay applicants were evaluated. We were granted a meeting with the head of the social service agency, along with some attorney friends of ours, in which we requested a written policy of non-discrimination to be crafted and incorporated into the consideration criteria for the fost/adopt program. And then we waited.

While waiting for social services to call, we also continued trying to conceive. When we parted ways with our prospective co-parents, we were directed to a woman who served as a go-between for men willing to donate and women wanting to conceive. The go-between was important, because we wanted to be sure that any prospective donor was unknown to us and had no claim to our child. The legal system at that time was granting parental rights to donors and we were wary of any potential consequences of direct donation. We used this woman's services several times, but with no success.

Finally we heard of a doctor and a nurse practitioner who were willing to help women conceive. Part of a general medical practice, they were supportive to the community, provided the "go-between" protection we wanted and were in a position to treat any possible fertility issues. We began trying to conceive with them in mid-1982 and continued to pursue our application to fost/adopt a child. On the conception side, we had several miscarriages and I began taking fertility drugs. On the fost/adopt side, we kept in touch with social services and closely monitored our status on the "list," as they called it.

In August 1983, we received a call from social services. They had a four-month-old boy who had been rejected by another fost/adopt family, because both of his parents were schizophrenic. Although initially concerned about his family background, we agreed to meet him and were instantly smitten. We knew we had found our baby.

Our son came home in September 1983, and we then began the eighteen-month process for me to become his legal mother. The same week our son arrived, I had another round of insemination scheduled. In addition to being on fertility drugs, we were also doing an intrauterine insemination in hopes of having a lasting pregnancy. In the excitement of the baby arriving, I forgot about the appointment and had to be reminded by a call from the doctor's office. I kept the appointment, the insemination was successful and nine months later, in June 1984, I gave birth to a baby girl.

The months between September 1983 and June 1984 were very hectic. Our son was still a foster child, so we felt a need to hide the pregnancy from our social worker for fear they might remove him. I always met with her sitting behind a table or holding my son in front of me. Our friends were astonished that we wanted two babies so close together and we received a lot of interest from women who wanted to know if we planned to give our son back if the new baby was a girl! This attitude was common at the time. I lived in fear that I might become the proud lesbian mother of multiple sons and an outcast in the community, because I had heard that fertility treatments often resulted in multiple births and insemination resulted in more male babies. I was so prepared to have a boy that when my daughter was born and the doctor told me she was a girl, I insisted he look again and show me, just to be sure.

Our daughter's birth certificate lists me as her only parent, because same-sex parents were not allowed in 1984. Our son's adoption eventually came through, although I was the only one able to adopt, since second-parent same-sex adoptions were not allowed either. My partner and I separated in 1989 and the only official record of her parenting relationship to our children was that they both have her last name as their middle names. There continues to be no legal bond between her and the children she helped create a family for. When we separated, we researched making her connection legal, but were told it was too early in the process to bring a test case where the parents' relationship had ended.

Although we both moved on to have other relationships, we continued to raise the children jointly and shared custody. The school years involved changing forms from "mother and father" to "parent and parent," the kids deciding which of their friends to "come out" to, which of us could be present at which event and us often navigating an unclear path of rules, regulations, preconceived notions and lack of knowledge. Through all of that, I believe I have learned as many lessons in understanding and tolerance as I may have taught. And over time, as the number of families like ours has increased and others have dedicated themselves to creating acceptance, that path has become much less difficult. Both of our kids graduated from a respected Catholic high school and went on to college. My son is now a social worker, dedicated to working with homeless inner-city youth. My daughter is a wife, mother and account manager at a major food supplier.

As my son prepared to graduate from high school with honors, I casually joked to a member of my congregation and a social worker that I thought I had proven I could do well with a foster child and was ready for another. Within weeks I met my next child, a twelve-year-old girl who had recently been orphaned. At the time, my son, daughter and I had recently moved into a house with my current partner. As a family, we agreed to meet this girl and decide if we thought she was a fit. They were all reluctant to move forward with bringing her into our family, but I strongly believed it was the right thing to do. She moved in shortly after her thirteenth birthday. This child is now twenty-six years old and has a master's degree in special education. Her adoption became final in 2010, with both my partner and I listed as her legal parents.

Our story is not over yet. I am now Nana to two beautiful grandchildren. My former partner remains as involved with them as she was with our own children, living with them and helping their parents juggle the demands of full-time work and parenting toddlers. My current spouse and I are also guardians to a wonderful fifteen-year-old boy who has been with us for the past six years. He is currently attending a Catholic all-boys high school, plays football and is the light of our lives.

When you do the math, we have three mothers, four children, one son-in-law and two grandchildren. The four children have four different biological mothers and two of them have three lesbian moms, one of which is also a biological mom. My grandchildren have two biological parents, one grandfather and four grandmothers. To some this may read like an algebra word problem, but to me, this is family.

# Rob Watson

SANTA CRUZ, CALIFORNIA

The issue was apparent the minute I came out as gay to my mother. I was twenty-four years old and completely unable to control my alcohol intake. That was what had driven me to this unplanned confessional. She, full of scorn, made the pronouncement as much a threat as a regret: "You have always wanted to be a dad. How can you be something that will keep you from ever being that?"

I don't remember what I said to her. I do know that I didn't have a real answer. Disclosing my orientation had nothing to do with my deep desire to have a family. I was drunk, I was angry and I was exposed. Her taunting inquiry did not shake my resolve. Yes, I was gay, but I was also going to live my life.

It was not until much later, after many years of sobriety and when I was safely in a relationship with a man I adored that the real answer to that question emerged: I was not going to be kept from being a dad. I just wasn't going to be a biological one.

My partner and I had briefly discussed having kids before, but the time had not been right. Then, suddenly it was. The question turned from whether we wanted to be parents to how. In this society, those who fight against marriage equality and marginalize gay people have lifted up biological procreation to be exalted. In their view, it is a sanctioned activity and those who can do it should reap extra legal rewards.

My own parents valued biological heritage and patriarchal tradition. Carrying on the family name was a noble cause. My father had researched and chronicled our family lineage going back three centuries. Since I was the only son, the continuation of him and our family branch was up to me. He only had a sister and none of her many children were going to carry the family name. Likewise, my sister's son and daughter, who bore many of his and my traits, didn't carry our surname, either.

I could give my kids the family name, but not our genetics. This made the legacy motivation to have children very confusing. Was it all about legal names? Or was it about passing down our traits, which were then watered down and watered down again with each generation? The moment I walked into the foster care orientation meeting, those questions became irrelevant. As I took my seat, the game shifted. I was no longer a name bearer and the need to propel my DNA forth through time ceased to be an issue.

Since my partner and I had past experiences with recovery from substance abuse, a process which created families from the wreckage of biological parents consumed by addiction seemed entirely appropriate. We knew the horrors and dysfunctions of alcohol and chemical abuse firsthand and held no judgment against those caught in its grip. We also felt enormous compassion for the innocents it threatened in its wake: the neglected and abused children of addicts. As we heard more about the process, we knew that being a part of this initiative was a clear mandate for us. The next few years were ones of preparation. We were trained, interrogated and inspected. Then we started to take temporary placements.

Cell phones were not as sophisticated as today's smartphones and it was the foster care system that first tied me to one of these devices. When a child entered the system, there was a list of ready families and the social worker went down the list until one of those families answered the call. Many of the cases were temporary, because the birthparents had made a mistake. With some training and commitment, they could reunite with their child.

Other cases were going to be permanent, however. The parents of these children were in the throes of seriously dangerous addictive behavior, or worse, and even the most basic reunification milestones were unattainable. In those cases, a different procreation occurred: A family became "with child" through the twinkling of a cell phone, rather than a night of heterosexual mating.

One day at work, my magic cell phone went off and when I answered, it was the procreation phone call of my family. A boy had been born. He was six weeks premature. His birthmother and father were heroin addicts and she had ingested the night before, sending her into labor.

I was told I could meet my new son that evening. The birthparents were informed of our arrival so they could step away from the care unit and let us see him alone. As I drove to the hospital, it felt like I was in a dream state. That morning I had just been a gay guy with a partner and now, that evening, I was finally becoming a dad.

The birthparents were not much into the rules. In spite of the request to give us a private moment with the baby, they were both there and greeted us at the door. It was shocking to meet them, not only because they were the birthparents of the child we were taking home the next day, but because they in no way looked like the people they had seemed to be on paper. I knew the nineteen-year-old birthmother had been addicted to heroin since she was sixteen and that it was her now-husband, two years older, who enticed her into first using the drug. They both had circulated on the street and with gangs.

But the people we saw before us did not project that history. They looked like sweet-faced teens. She was in a fluffy pink bathrobe, her beautiful hair pulled back into a ponytail. He was kind and attentive.

They did not have my attention for long. My focus was on the baby in the clear plastic incubator bed with IVs attached to his tiny extremities. Despite all the medical apparatus, he was beautiful. The baby had gotten most of the heroin out of his system and only needed painkillers for another day. I marveled at the human being I saw before me and wondered what natural survival mode could have propelled him to leave his mother's body so early and free himself of those foreign narcotics.

We chatted with his birthparents for a long while. They were amazingly traditional and ordinary. There were only a few telltale signs that they came from a different world. One was their litany of friends who had lost their children to the protective care system. The couple quizzed us as to whether we knew this child or that. Quietly I shook my head and wondered what it was like to be in a social environment where those separations were commonplace.

The nurse brought my new son over in a blanket and I held him softly on my chest. I looked into his eyes and we connected. He was home; I was home. This was right. Deep in my heart, I knew this child was my son forever. He was named Jason. Loving, protecting and defending him was now my life's calling. While I dutifully listened and took down instructions like an evening babysitter, I knew I was embarking on the love of my life. I was a father. My son had fought his battle getting into this world and now it was up to me to help him the rest of the way. He never had to fight alone again.

As I have shared stories of my family since that time, some people have claimed I did my son a disservice by being his father and a gay dad. They have asserted that depriving Jason of his birthparents was an act of violence against him. I understand that some groups petitioned advertisers to get *The Fosters,* a television program that depicts a family like mine, off the air. They think we are dangerous.

But the birthparents were given over a year to get their act together and prepare themselves to raise a baby with special needs. They never spent much of that time bonding with Jason and he never actually knew them as parents. The birthmother went on to bear several more drug-exposed babies over the next few years, each one more severely exposed than the last. The birthfather ended up in prison. Neither kicked their heroin addiction and there were rumors that both had died of overdoses.

I carried Jason in a sling on my chest for his first few months of life. He slept on my heartbeat. We had specific challenges to accomplish for him in terms of nourishment, keeping him calm, sleeping with and swaddling him to create security. Each of these was required for him to successfully develop into a healthy toddler.

The intimacy of this process—our hearts so closely aligned, my daily, hourly prayers going into him and my dreams enveloping his—created a bond deeper than I had ever imagined. I can easily say this bond was greater than any I could have had with a child I biologically fathered. As Jason grew plump and healthy, our family flourished and our household exuded joy.

When Jason approached a year and a half in age, we began taking calls for placements again. We were now envisioning child number two—the final member of our little family. We were awaiting another impregnating phone call. I had imagined a little girl for our second child—a tiny moppet who looked up to and was protected by her big brother, mirroring my own experience with my "baby sister."

We got that call. She was a beautiful baby girl and looked just like Jason did when he was a newborn. However, it became evident that she wasn't going to fit in our family puzzle. Life had other plans for her and even better plans for us.

The baby girl's birthmother was responding well to the recovery program. This was actually a thrilling development and even though it seemed disruptive to our own plan, it was an honor to be a part of that unification. We cheered as the young mother cleaned up her life in preparation for giving her daughter a safe and productive childhood. We supported that momentum and looked forward to a happy mother-and-daughter reunion.

Meanwhile, another foster family who were good friends of ours recently had a ten-month-old boy placed with them. The boy had been discovered abandoned in a trailer. My partner often took Jason to their home on playdates and the little boy and my son became very close.

The two seemed to speak a common language and played well together. My partner called me at work one day and said, "You have to come see this little boy and how he and Jason are. I told the other family to let us know if there was any problem with their placement, because we would love to take him in." I was alright with this, but remained a little guarded as this had not been our original plan. However, plans change and life takes over.

When I got home that evening, the playdate was still going on. I'll never forget the moment I first saw Jesse: He was crawling around the corner headed toward the dishwasher as I was coming the other way. We locked eyes. It was one of the most profound moments of my life. The look between us said it all.

*Hi, Dad. I'm your son.*

*Hi, Jesse. I'm going to be your dad.*

A week later, it happened. The foster mother called and asked if we were serious about our offer. It turns out that her family had to move into some tight temporary quarters. She was much better equipped to care for the baby that my partner and I were currently nursing than Jesse, the rough-and-tumble toddler. So we called the authorities and made the switch. Jason and Jesse, new best friends, were now on their way to potentially becoming brothers.

Being the working dad, however, I was worried that I might not get to bond with Jesse as I had with Jason. My feelings for Jason were deep and thorough. I felt he had emerged and grown right out of my heart and nothing on earth could take that away.

I was not going to carry Jesse on me for months. I saw him in the mornings before I left for work and in time for a kiss goodnight when I returned. He was exposed to my partner and other foster care providers more than he was seeing me. More to the point, reunification with his birthfather was also in full swing and there was a very good chance we might not be Jesse's permanent home after all.

The plan had progressed to weekend visits with the birthfather. We were supportive, but Jesse was coming home with an air of urgency, desperate to be back with us. One weekend, things went horribly awry.

My partner called me in a panic. He had picked Jesse up from the birthfather's house and saw that the boy had been badly bruised and possibly beaten. My partner drove him directly to the social worker. I got a follow-up call soon after that: Jesse had bruises where no two-year-old should have them. These bruises were from no normal rough and tumble. The reunification plan came to a screeching halt. Jesse was home, ours forever, but we now had a clearly traumatized little boy who was unable to tell us exactly what had happened.

I slept in the same room with Jesse for the next two weeks. The little boy who normally slept soundly through the night woke screaming almost hourly. I held him, comforted him and cried with him. I enveloped him with every stretch of my soul, trying to erase and dissolve the pain and fear. "Daddy's here, little one. Daddy's here. No one is going to get to you again, I swear it."

Jesse quickly recovered and our family was made whole. We had been created. Our building blocks were not physical; they were much bigger than that. Our family was built with substances that were spiritual and psychic, elements that broke the bounds of emotion. Our family is realer than real and the experience of it coming into existence has surpassed any superficial experience I could have imagined or designed on my own.

We have discussed their biological parents and the addiction that they have had to deal with. Jason and Jesse have seen pictures and understand their birthparents deal with diseases that make them incapable of caring for children. Our kids are both aware of their biological heritage and we answer questions in depth as they have them.

Today, I look at two boys. They are two brothers, almost twins. They share and speak a language unto themselves. I am their dad as much as, if not more than, anyone is anyone's dad on the planet. As I look at them, I recognize the two different parts of myself that brought them into being—neither of which was part of my personal biology.

Jason is the child of my heart. Jesse is the child of my soul. It was in each where the translucent but iron link between us was forged. If that is not procreation, I don't know what is.

# Thomas Whaley and Carl Leichthammer

SHOREHAM, NEW YORK

From the dawn of our relationship, which began in the winter of 2000, Carl and I both knew that we wanted children. Our initial conversations about the hopes of fatherhood were casual, often preceded with "One day..." We were young, spontaneous and just beginning our teaching careers, so it was not our main focus, but rather a dream. As time went by and our love and respect for each other grew stronger, we celebrated by having a commitment ceremony in October of 2002. We knew a family was going to follow eventually, but like any other newlyweds, we had no idea when. We decided to wait for the "right moment," but honestly, is there ever one?

Carl and I agreed that we wanted a house before adding children into the mix. Commitment, house and then children. The order seemed so 1950s traditional, but we enjoyed calling ourselves the "unconventional traditional couple," so this order worked for us. Once we settled into our new home in 2005, we decided the time was right to make our dream of becoming parents a reality. We had no idea how exhausting and difficult the initial process was going to be.

First we weighed all the available options. Surrogacy was enticing, but also extremely expensive, and neither of us felt that biology was important. Foster care scared us: We cringed at the idea of becoming emotionally attached to a child and then possibly having to hand him or her back to someone knocking on our front door.

Adopting children from other countries was another one of our choices, but most countries at the time did not allow LGBT couples to adopt. We knew adopting in the United States was the right choice for us and eventually found the right adoption agency to work with. In the winter of 2006, we attended the agency's "get acquainted" weekend and officially embarked on the process of starting our family.

We were not ready for the emotional rollercoaster it turned out to be! Looking back, we now laugh, roll our eyes and often wonder how we survived the initial stages of the adoption. All couples, gay or straight, should receive a gold star just for this part of the process: fingerprints, background checks, job and social histories, past addresses, bank statements, home visits, lawyer fees, 800-numbers and creating a brochure and website. It all seemed tedious and endless, but the encouragement from our friends and family kept our eyes on the prize—a beautiful child to call our own and complete our family.

After five months, New York State decided we were fit to adopt and ready to be picked. It was at this precise moment that we were gently reminded by our assigned agency counselor that it could take as long as five years to be chosen by a birthmother. So like many other couples "in waiting," we got a dog—a yellow lab puppy named Jake.

Waiting was difficult at times. Carl and I made sure to communicate our feelings throughout the process, both with each other and with family and friends. During our waiting period, several of our close friends became pregnant and had babies. As much as we wanted to rejoice, we often found ourselves feeling jealous or depressed, which was an awful way to feel, especially since those feelings were new for both of us. Luckily, we were very close with our friends Keith and Peter, who had also begun the process of adopting, so the four of us could sit down and relate to one another, which made our rollercoaster of emotions easier to bear. Our adoption agency also had counselors on staff who called to check up on us. They were always available to talk.

As time went by, many postcards from our adoption agency came to our home, each one briefly outlining a woman who requested our boastful brochure. They didn't excite us as much as we wanted them to. But one summer day in 2007, a postcard came that made us curiously giddy. It called out to us: This birthmother was not a teenager, it was not her first child and she was a professional. As much as we didn't want to stereotype, she seemed like someone who knew adoption was right for her. It was the first and only one we posted on our fridge.

For months we stared at the postcard, waiting for our phone to ring. And one day it did. But it was not a call that we expected. It was the Department of Health and Human Services (DHHS) in Tacoma,

Washington. They had a three-month-old baby boy in foster care and his birthparents' rights were about to be terminated. They explained that if things worked out, it might be quite a while before he could come home.

Two weeks later, we were on a plane to meet Andrew. We spent the holidays with him. We fell in love with him. And even though we had to leave without him, we got home and began preparing for Andrew's pending arrival. We called our adoption agency and took ourselves off the waiting list until we were ready to adopt again. We took down the postcard and celebrated New Year's Eve with an entirely different outlook on life. We were going to be dads.

Just days after celebrating the New Year, our hopes of becoming Andrew's fathers were shattered: "I'm so sorry. You cannot adopt Andrew. His mother has agreed to go into a treatment facility, so we cannot terminate her rights." It was what we feared the most about adopting through foster care. The emotions we felt were catastrophic. It took two days and many boxes of tissues before we could call our adoption agency and ask them to put us back on the waiting list. We felt defeated. We took the postcard out of the drawer next to the fridge and put it back up. It helped us feel that hope again.

On January 6th, 2008, we were back on the waiting list. The next day we got a call from the birthmother on the postcard. She had chosen us when we were at our lowest point!

Our future son's birthmother invited us to her sonogram one week after we first spoke. It was amazing! We drove deep into the heart of Pennsylvania and stayed overnight. The sonogram experience was more than we could have ever asked for and seeing the baby for the very first time left us speechless. We had never imagined having sonogram pictures to share with our friends and family. During our time together after the sonogram, we went shopping with the birthmother for some comfortable maternity clothes and got to meet her two sons.

A few months later, we drove back to Pennsylvania to help deliver our son, Luke Thomas. He was perfect and his birthmother was our guardian angel. On April 14th, my birthday, we were allowed to bring Luke home with us. Knowing his birthmother had sixty days to change her mind was bothersome at times, but greatly overpowered by the love we both felt for our son. Calling each other Dad or Daddy was amazing. Even though we were aware of the sixty-day window, in our hearts we knew he was our son for life. And even though we were overwhelmed with lack of sleep, lawyers, paperwork and follow-up home visits, it didn't seem to be bothersome anymore.

The communication with Luke's birthmother afterward was consistent—we spoke with her several times a week. We really got to know each other well during the pregnancy and ended up becoming friends. We even connected with her on social media and she has been watching Luke grow up through the pictures we post. It has been a great way for her to feel good about her decision, knowing he is well taken care of and living a happy life.

Even though everything was going well, one thing still bothered us—Andrew. One day we got an urgent phone message: "Hello, Tom and Carl. This is DHHS. We have something very important and exciting to share with you. Please call us when you get a chance." We found out that Andrew's mother had dropped out of the rehabilitation program and that her parental rights had been terminated. Andrew was ours. On July 5th, Carl's birthday, Andrew came home and completed our family.

Our boys are now six years old. Andrew's birthmother made some amazing, positive life changes in that time and we have since reestablished contact with her. Andrew even mailed her a card that he had made in school and we set up a phone conversation on Mother's Day right after Luke spoke with his birthmother. Both boys now have that in common and can talk with each other about their feelings and excitement.

Adoption paperwork, background checks, lawyers, home visits and sleepless nights have now been replaced with lacrosse, soccer and basketball practices, video games, homework, arguing over chores and taking care of our two dogs, Jake and Sam. We are a hectic house of six. Every step along the way has grounded us, humbled us. It made us stronger as a couple and now as a family.

We began our journey with hopes of finding our babies, but our babies ended up finding us.

# Lisa Blake and Kerry Booth

DERBY, UNITED KINGDOM

Time seems to have flown and I can't work out whether I feel a million years older with children in my life or as youthful and energetic as a puppy. At thirty-something, my partner and I decided to begin an application to become foster parents for social services. We chose the foster care route over one of us physically giving birth for a number of reasons: there were so many children out there needing good homes and we didn't feel "the need" or that maternal yearning to give birth ourselves. Also, we were both too squeamish!

Having a house with a little extra room, steady jobs and a solid relationship, Kerry and I felt that we were ready for something more and could offer a child the love and support, comfort and security desperately needed by so many. A number of our family and friends had commented that we "ought to do it" and that we'd "make great parents," so one fresh New Year back in 2010, after much consideration, we finally did.

For most couples in a heterosexual relationship, having children in their lives is often something that "just happens." It's socially and culturally accepted as the norm and therefore expected and encouraged. However, Kerry and I gave the prospect a lot of thought. We had both become very comfortable with each other and enjoyed our lifestyle of freedom and spontaneity. How might things change with a third or even fourth presence in our calm and peaceful home?

Our family and circle of friends were supportive and encouraging and any of our work colleagues who may have been against it on religious grounds didn't voice any ill wishes. Curiously, it was my mother—known to berate me with "I'll never be a grandmother" remarks—who was the most disgruntled about it. However, since my lack of heterosexuality has disappointed and disgruntled my mother through most of my "out" life, I'm beginning to let it roll off my shoulders now.

The application went in and our first visit from the assessing social worker was arranged. She was a lovely lady with a thousand questions.

Over countless cups of tea (milk, no sugar), she recorded what seemed like our entire life history, including our childhood upbringing, family members, our relationship and medical background. It seemed like a lot to delve into, but Kerry and I understood it was important. Our homosexuality was discussed briefly, but in an honest and pragmatic way. The social worker had to know that we were prepared for anything.

"How would you feel if a child asked if you were gay? How might you respond if a child saw you holding hands or being affectionate?" she asked politely.

These questions may seem intrusive at first and the temptation for many is to fire back another question: "Are these the questions you ask straight couples?" But the fact is that social workers need to get to know the people who are potentially being allowed to bring vulnerable children into their homes and lives. They have to get it right. Failure here is catastrophic for a child in any situation, heterosexual or homosexual. Assessing social workers may or may not ask straight people similar questions, but it's true that many children may have preconceived ideas about what relationships and families are like.

At the risk of us sounding like "the only gays in the county," it was important for the social worker to hear us respond thoughtfully, honestly, positively and appropriately to the child's age and be aware of any preconceived and possibly negative views he or she may have from previous life experiences. I felt our social worker supported us at every step and that our calm but positive opinions on equal rights and diversity worked well within the fostering network's ethos.

Several more interviews and many more cups of tea went by over the coming months, including standard interviews with our parents, other family members and close friends. We had health and safety checks on the house, garden and cars and even a "Cat Questionnaire" to determine any risk factors that may arise with our two little moggies!

As summer drew to a close, September arrived and it was back to school for Kerry and I. We had three weekends of foster care training that month. Despite a few grumbles at the thought of "working weekends" and a mounting folder of material to read and respond to, we marched on, feeling more than ever that this is what we wanted to do. I remember the first day of training. There was a mixture of people there, all with welcoming smiles, nods and pleasantries. We helped ourselves to tea and sat down in two of the chairs set out in a large circle.

"Hello and thank you for coming," the trainer began. "I know that you'd all probably rather be tucked up in bed at this time on a Saturday morning." She set the tone for what became a warm-hearted and fun training session. First up, however, were the introductions. "Let's go around the circle introducing ourselves and what age group you might be looking at fostering."

Kerry has always been pretty confident about being openly gay, but hated any form of public speaking. I, being a teacher, had grown somewhat better at public speaking, but had struggled for years to talk confidently about being gay! Every other couple in the group was heterosexual. *Never mind. Be brave, Lisa,* I told myself. I'm learning that "coming out" is not a one-off. It's an ongoing, lifelong scenario I have to get used to.

I introduced myself and spoke of our interest in looking after children on a respite basis—some weekends and school holidays to fit around work commitments—with a preference for newborns to five-year-olds. I finished by saying, "And this is my partner of several years, Kerry." Introductions done! No gasps from the audience, no shocked expressions. Any private thoughts were not aired. We felt good and, I have to admit, a little bit relieved, too.

By early 2011, our foster care application was ready to be handed to a panel of counselors, experienced foster parents, committee members, the Head of Fostering Services and a number of other officials and professionals. By that time, we had been assigned a supporting social worker who guided us through each stage of the process. The big day arrived and Kerry and I made our way to the local Fostering and Adoption Head Office to face the panel.

The anticipation was slightly apprehensive and the occasion quite formal, with a panel of a dozen people sitting around a large oval table—our application in front of them—and deciding whether or not we were fit to look after children. However, after a few simple questions and a more informal conversation than I had expected, our application was supported unanimously and we were approved as foster parents.

We didn't have to wait long before our supporting social worker came for her routine monthly visit with news of a little girl in need of respite care on a regular basis. That May, the little seven-year-old had her first visit with us and three years later, she is still visiting every other weekend. At bedtime for the first several visits she had a few tears, because she missed her home. Now she can't wait to come and arrives bounding in with nuclear energy. Last year she wanted to stay for Christmas and even wants to call us both Mummy. Our two little cats find new hiding places every other weekend and our calm, peaceful home life gets turned upside down as it's given the exuberant gift of youth each fortnight.

Since our first panel meeting, we have fostered several other children and attended annual panel review meetings. The children and families we supported have responded positively towards us as caregivers. I believe we've had the opportunity to truly share our lives, being visible in our diversity and demonstrating "normal" family life and a "normal" positive and supportive relationship. Furthermore, we are now approved to foster two children from newborn to eighteen years of age on a respite or intermediate basis. More recently, we have been asked to be foster care mentors to support newly approved foster parents beginning their journey towards fostering and maybe even adoption.

The inevitable question of sexuality arose one day when one of our children asked, "Are you girlfriend and girlfriend?"

Quite simply and honestly, we replied with age-appropriate awareness: "Yes, some girls love boys, some girls love girls and some boys love boys. We love each other just like any other husband and wife."

"Are you gay?" the little girl continued.

"Yes, some people say 'lesbian,' some people say 'gay,'" we replied pragmatically. "Either way, we just know that we love each other and that's okay."

As Kerry's grandmother once said, "You can't help who you fall in love with."

At one point, we looked after a wonderful two-year-old girl and had her in our care for over eighteen months. Kerry and I hoped to adopt her, but that was not to be on this occasion, as she eventually went to live with her birthfamily. The council's policy of "keeping families together" mandates that children should be with their birthfamily members wherever appropriate.

Although this sweet girl has moved on to her new home now, she still makes us little creations at her nursery and drew a portrait of Kerry and me. We are still in touch with her and she will always have a special place in our hearts. Her portrait is the most wonderful thing I've ever seen and it made both Kerry and I very emotional. The girl turned four recently and has progressed so much. To have played a big part in her development has been the most rewarding thing we have ever done as a couple.

Kerry and I have found ourselves once again enjoying the freedoms and pleasures of life together, but never rule out fostering or adoption possibilities in the future. We know for sure now that we could give a child a wonderful life.

# PART 3
# SURROGACY

A surrogate is a woman who carries and gives birth to a child on behalf of another person or couple. There are two types of surrogacy: traditional and gestational.

With *traditional* surrogacy, the surrogate is also the egg donor, meaning that she is the biological mother of the child. She is typically impregnated through a process known as intrauterine insemination (IUI), where sperm from the biological father is transferred into her uterus. With *gestational* surrogacy, the surrogate and egg donor are not the same person, which means the surrogate is not biologically related to the child. In this scenario, pregnancy is achieved through a process called in vitro fertilization (IVF), where the donor egg is fertilized in a laboratory prior to being transferred into the surrogate's uterus. It is important to note that every state that protects families who utilize surrogacy requires the gestational method.

Surrogacy agencies help match prospective parents with potential surrogate mothers. During the matching phase, future parents and surrogates interview each other to make sure everyone has the same intentions for the surrogacy journey. How much contact and communication do they want before and after birth? Will there be any dietary restrictions? Do the future parents want to attend doctor visits?

Once there is a match, all parties involved set expectations and sign contracts in the beginning. This normally makes for a harmonious experience for everyone involved, but that's not to say there are no challenges or complications. Surrogates have to go through a lot of medically invasive procedures and these procedures can sometimes be difficult and uncomfortable. It can also take multiple attempts to conceive and miscarriages are common in these types of pregnancies. It is important that you speak with a medical professional to get a clear understanding of the potential complications that could arise.

One of the benefits of surrogacy is that you have the opportunity to witness and be a part of the pregnancy journey. You can be present for sonograms, the baby's first heartbeat and even the birth. All of that comes with a price, though. When taking into consideration the cost of hiring a surrogate, possibly paying a portion of the surrogate mother's living expenses, the cost of the medical procedures, agency fees, lawyer fees and more, you're looking at somewhere over $100,000. On top of that, many insurance companies will not cover the costs of the fertilization or delivery when using a surrogate. Surrogacy is by far the most expensive journey to parenthood.

Because of the large sums of money involved, you need to make sure you're not being taken advantage of. There are plenty of scams that prey on unsuspecting people with dreams of building a family. Make sure you research potential agencies thoroughly prior to working with one. Don't make your decision based on a well-designed website or the testimonials found there. Ask for references so that you can speak directly to people who have been through the program. Contact independent physicians, attorneys and mental health professionals for objective opinions about the agency and program you are considering. Also, make sure to seek the advice of an independent attorney who can oversee the process and advocate on your behalf.

This section of the book explains what it is like for people in the LGBT community to go through the surrogacy journey. It also compares domestic and international surrogacy and provides examples of unexpected things that can occur along the way. For instance, what happens if a foreign government makes it complicated for you to get a birth certificate and passport for your child after he or she is born outside of the United States? What is the process like for people who live in states that make it difficult for LGBT couples to adopt? And for those of you who want to know how men in same-sex relationships might decide which one is going to biologically father the child…well, that's covered too.

# David and Josh

WEST PALM BEACH, FLORIDA

When talking about how they became parents, gay people often describe it in terms of being on a journey. This is an understandable metaphor, because the process of becoming a parent as a gay person is often a long, complicated and uncertain undertaking with a highly desired outcome at the end. In our own situation, we have found the term to be entirely appropriate as well, as our journey to parenthood has taken us across the country and eventually around the world.

Josh and I met in our home state of New York and have been together since 1997. From the early days of our relationship, we liked to escape the crowded city on weekend getaways and have earnest conversations in the car about our future while gazing out on the open road. Josh comes from a large and close extended family and has always wanted children. I wanted children too, but was more reserved about it, because I have always taught myself not to long too hard for something that's unlikely to come to fruition. It was the 1990s. Gay men having babies together was still exceedingly rare.

Josh moved to Florida in 1999 to help out with a family business and I followed shortly thereafter as soon as I finished school. We suddenly found ourselves in a state that was rather hostile to gay people and still had laws on the books dating back to the days of anti-gay activist Anita Bryant, such as one that specifically forbade gays to adopt. Circumstances did not appear favorable, but Josh was undeterred and did his own research about our options. In 2005, he came across a book about gay fathers that described the process of surrogacy in California. We learned that it was possible to work with a woman who could undergo in vitro fertilization (IVF) and carry a baby for us.

If the donated eggs did not come from the surrogate, but rather an anonymous donor, it was possible to go to a California court prior to the birth and have maternity declared to be "in doubt." Then both of our names could be recorded as parents on the birth documents. After a great deal of discussion, we made a trip out to California to visit an agency that specialized in surrogacy with gay clientele. My enthusiasm grew.

Circumstances appeared to align perfectly with the temporarily insane American housing market telling us that the modest home we purchased a few years earlier was worth twice that amount in 2006. So we took out a home equity line of credit and set up a trust to fund the expensive IVF process. This method of paying for the first leg of our journey meant that we were younger and of more limited means than most of the agency's clients. We discovered that typical surrogacy clients were either independently wealthy or had been saving up for many years.

We were paying top dollar for a concierge-type service and the agency in California carefully coordinated the process from beginning to end. They connected us with a prestigious IVF doctor in Beverly Hills, had their lawyers prepare our case for the family court process and compiled a large database of potential egg donors for us to select from.

Because I'm of Asian descent and Josh is Jewish, we always planned to have mixed race children who might hopefully reflect both of our heritages. To that end, we sifted through the numerous blonde Hollywood headshots to find profiles of Asian and Jewish egg donors. We selected the egg donor we felt had qualities we wanted in our children, like a keen intellect and strong career aspirations. Then we contributed the complementary sperm donation from our side of the equation to make the embryos for implantation. We have always chosen to keep the exact genetics of our situation confidential, because we both want to be treated equally as parents. Even though plenty of people have come to their own conclusions along the way about what happened, the fact that we have neither confirmed nor denied the specifics has introduced enough doubt to keep the speculators at bay. Besides, we have always felt the children should be the first to know about their true genetic heritage when they are old enough to understand.

Josh has always said that the one part of the process the agency in California really aced was matching us with our surrogate, Marie. We filled out lengthy questionnaires and constructed an introductory profile of ourselves, describing our hopes and expectations. The agency searched their pool of carefully screened prospective surrogates for women with similar expectations and presented our profile to make a match. Marie has told us that we were not the first profile sent her way, but the first she agreed to, because Josh and I were relatively young and seemed sturdy enough for the task of parenting.

The agency arranged a meeting for Marie and us in October 2006. We hit it off immediately. She was a military wife raising two small children and she lived with her husband, who was stationed on a base outside San Diego. We have joked that what followed was a typical whirlwind "military romance," because Josh and I were parents by July 2007.

Coincidentally, Marie was cycling in synchrony with our chosen egg donor, so the egg retrieval, fertilization and embryo transfer were all scheduled within days after we accepted Marie as our surrogate. A month later, we were back on a plane to California. On the big day of the embryo transfer, our IVF doctor told us that only a few embryos had developed, but the ones that did were of good quality. This meant that we didn't have enough embryos left over to freeze and try for a second cycle if the first transfer didn't take.

Knowing that we might have to start the egg donor selection all over again if our first try was unsuccessful, we decided to take the "all in" approach and transfer the maximum number of embryos allowed by the doctor: three. We felt capable of handling a single baby or twins, but planned to reduce the pregnancy in the event of triplets, because high-order pregnancies are risky and we were not gambling with our own bodies, but with Marie's. Luckily, we didn't have to make that hard decision: Over the holidays, we were blessed with the news that Marie was pregnant with twins!

Over the course of the next several months, Josh and I took turns traveling from Florida to California to attend medical visits and spend time with Marie and her family. We both attended an OB/GYN appointment early in the second trimester for a 3D ultrasound and learned that we were expecting two boys. On the last weekend of June, Josh went out to California to attend the thirty-two-week ultrasound and everything seemed to be on track with the pregnancy. He finalized plans with a hotel to check in for one month near the due date and after a walk-through at the hospital maternity ward, he took a red-eye flight back to Florida on Sunday night. I picked him up at the airport early Monday morning so we could both go to work. By the time we were getting ready for dinner on Monday night, we received a call from California that something was amiss.

Marie had noticed a light sensation in her chest earlier that day after doing some housework, but she attributed it to stress and fatigue from the activities of the preceding weekend (aside from Josh, she also had family in town). She went on about her day and drove herself to a scheduled OB/GYN visit, only for the doctor to discover that she was in ventricular tachycardia with a very rapid heartbeat. The OB/GYN ordered her to the hospital immediately and a team of doctors tried decreasing her heart rate, but the medications they used seemed to be inducing preterm labor at thirty-two weeks. We received the phone call feeling powerless, learning that an emergency C-section was becoming inevitable—and we were not going to be there.

JJ and AJ were born and immediately transferred to the neonatal intensive care unit (NICU). We booked the earliest flight we could find to go back to California on Tuesday morning—it was the very same plane Josh had just flown on twenty-four hours prior. We rushed directly to the hospital and checked with Marie to see that she was recovering well before meeting our sons for the first time. Upon receipt of the legal paperwork from the agency, the hospital staff was very kind and treated us like any other parents visiting their children in the NICU. The nurses took our picture and placed it in the incubator isolettes so JJ and AJ could become familiar with gazing at their new parents.

Then the nurses proceeded to give us a wonderful crash course in caring for premature infants, including everything from feeding issues to tiny diaper changes. We spent the next five weeks camped out in an extended-stay hotel close to the hospital, visiting every few hours to participate in feeding and baby care. Marie had graciously agreed to pump breast milk to help the twins, so we also served as the "milk men," picking up frozen bottles from the military base and shuttling them to the NICU so we could thaw the milk and feed it to the boys.

Our sons had a few typical preemie issues with feeding and breathing, so when the boys were finally discharged from the hospital in early August, they were sent home with apnea monitors strapped to their chests to ensure their breathing remained regular. We were instructed to spike their bottles with pharmaceutical caffeine to ensure they never fell into a deep enough sleep where they forgot to breathe. A week after being released from the hospital, the boys were cleared to fly. We said our goodbyes and left California to come back home to Florida. However, we still remain in contact with Marie to this day. Whenever we post photos of the boys on social media, she or her mother are usually the first to comment!

The first few months at home with the boys were challenging, to say the least. Josh and I foolishly tried to juggle premature twins on our own while maintaining full-time jobs (albeit with alternating schedules) and nearly drove ourselves insane during the process. Coaxing a bottle into one of the twins could take as long as an hour, so there was very little downtime and it felt nearly continuous alternating between one twin who was feeding and the other who was screaming with hunger. We were constantly tripping over the apnea monitors, which felt like balls and chains. After three months, the boys learned how to kick the wires loose and we had a few early morning false alarms erupt through the house before we retired the monitors to the closet.

By November, we were ready to wave the white flag when Josh's mother told us about a conversation that she had struck up with a nanny caring for twins and an older brother at the local mall. It turned out that the nanny, Pat, was looking for a new job, because the children she was caring for were moving out of state. Pat started working with us eight hours a day and was a dream, caring for the boys all the way up until they started preschool at age three.

When JJ and AJ were four years old in 2012, I distinctly recall a moment on one of our frequent family trips to nearby theme parks in Florida. I sat down to rest and watched the boys run off to play in the distance. They were becoming more and more independent. I felt weariness in my bones, my subconscious calculations became conscious and I realized we were running out of time.

A few weeks later, on a weekend getaway to New York to celebrate our fifteenth anniversary, I explained to Josh over a romantic dinner that ever since the boys were born, I had been constantly adding eighteen to our ages. If we had another child right then, how old was I going to be before they were all grown up? I confessed to Josh my yearning for another child on that trip. Josh was not as sure this time around, but decided to go along for the ride. We began to plan for our next journey together.

Times had changed and the economy of 2012 was not nearly as conducive to baby making. We made furtive communication with the agency in California, only to find that financing an identical process five years later was now going to be much more difficult. We had paid off the line of credit and I had a job that paid more, but Josh's business was not doing nearly as well as it was during the boom years and banks were no longer giving the type of credit that had been our ace in the hole back in 2006.

However, Josh's research saved the day yet again when he came across the concept of international surrogacy. Following the lead of agencies like the one in California, operations were springing up in Latin America and Asia that offered gestational surrogacy at much lower costs compared to the United States. We began investigating our international options. After briefly considering Latin America, we ultimately honed in on India, because it offered modern medicine on par with US standards—but at lower costs—as well as a relatively cosmopolitan setting to locate an egg donor of Caucasian or Asian descent.

In selecting the specific Indian clinic, our prior experience as parents through surrogacy served us well in weeding out some questionable situations. In some cases, we knew immediately that we were being lied to. "No need to make the trip to India beforehand," one clinic said. "We can just ship your stuff to India, because frozen is as good as fresh for IVF." That was a lie. "To ensure success in one cycle, we can transfer to two different surrogates. I know you just said you would prefer a singleton. The two surrogates have never gotten pregnant at the same time like that, and certainly not with multiples." Another lie. We eliminated those agencies making false promises and quickly whittled down our options to an American facilitator who had gone through the surrogacy process in India himself and was referring people directly to a clinic in Mumbai.

Some claims were not as easily disproven. We had to see the operation for ourselves to make sure everything was legit. In October 2012, my sister, Annie, and brother-in-law, Rahul, came to Florida to stay for ten days, so they could take JJ and AJ to school and go trick-or-treating with them on Halloween while Josh and I made our first trip to India. We were very quiet about our plans, because we felt there was a lot of uncertainty pursuing international surrogacy. Not many people knew we were even going to be away. We didn't want it to be public knowledge if we were about to be swindled.

Once we met with the clinic director, we felt comfortable enough to proceed. We got the sense that the clinic director genuinely cared for the welfare of her surrogates. She introduced us to the person we were going to potentially match with. Because of language and cultural barriers, we knew that this relationship could never be like the one we had with Marie. However, when a translator informed our new surrogate that we had selected her, the beaming smile on her face told us that she was very happy for this opportunity.

Because of different economies in the US versus India, the fee that we had paid Marie was certainly nice, but nothing she couldn't make working for several months at any number of jobs. Even though the money we gave to our surrogate in India was a fraction of that amount, in the Indian economy this money was life-changing for her family and could actually buy her a home or put both of her own children through school. We dove into the IVF process again, using an egg donor we had selected via e-mail correspondence prior to the trip. Before our return to the US, we politely asked to limit the number of embryos transferred on this first try to just two, because we wanted to aim for a singleton. Apparently, fate decided we could handle more than that. A few weeks later, we received an e-mail announcing that we were pregnant with twins…again.

Because of logistical issues, our dozen trips to California to visit with Marie were reduced to two visits to India: one for baby making and one for baby pickup. In the months between, we had to satisfy ourselves with relatively infrequent and curt e-mails announcing the basic status of things with ultrasound pictures every month or so. This sparse communication proved unnerving at times and nagging doubts sometimes emerged. What if we were being swindled after all? We had recurring nightmares of returning to India only to find the infertility clinic had been suddenly replaced with a nail salon and none of the nail techs knew anything about babies.

We asked for some guidance about the projected delivery date and decided to go to Mumbai a bit early to avoid any surprises that might cause us to miss the birth like we did the first time. We ended up spending the second half of June waiting in Mumbai, camped out in a hotel and planning different permutations of baby names. Determining the baby's gender prior to birth was illegal in India, so we didn't know if we were ending up with boys, girls or one of each.

Baby girl DJ and baby boy MJ ended up being born, by coincidence, on the day before their older brothers' birthday, but much closer to full-term at thirty-seven weeks. They did not have the prematurity issues that JJ and AJ had, so they were discharged uneventfully after three days in a regular hospital room and we took them back to our hotel.

The phase of international surrogacy that we had always anticipated to be the most difficult was getting the necessary paperwork to bring our children home to the US. After spending only a few days in India with Josh and the babies to get the process rolling—and with work responsibilities and the older twins waiting at home—I headed back to the US while Josh and the little ones waited for the proper travel documents to be issued. We had estimates that it could take anywhere from two weeks to two months.

We each effectively became single parents of twins on opposite sides of the globe. I jumped right back into full-time work, dropping off JJ and AJ each day at summer camp. Given his experience and night-owl tendencies, Josh didn't have too much trouble handling the infants overnight on his own at the hotel. During the daytime, we hired a nurse from an agency recommended by the hospital to help care for the twins so Josh could rest and get some work done. Again, due to the economic differences, a nurse to care for the twins eleven hours a day only ended up costing the equivalent of fifty US dollars. It was well worth it and the nurse was a wonderful help.

The first step right after the birth was making an appointment at the US Consulate in Mumbai to apply for a Consular Report of Birth Abroad (CRBA). To submit this application, we had to provide multiple documents and DNA samples to show that DJ and MJ are the biological children of a US citizen who has lived in the US for at least five years. This proved that DJ and MJ are natural-born US citizens who acquired their citizenship at birth, no matter what the anti-DJ-or-MJ-for-president birthers of 2056 will have to say.

The supporting evidence was all conscientiously gathered for the big day, only for us to find out that the US Consulate's credit card machine was temporarily down and that we needed to pay in cash. After a mad scramble in a taxi searching for a bank that could advance cash on a US-based card, the taxi driver ended up saving the day by driving to his own home nearby and fronting us the cash to be paid back after returning to the hotel on the other side of Mumbai, over an hour away. Phew!

After more than a week of anxiously waiting for the application materials to be sent to the US for processing, DJ and MJ were officially declared US citizens and passports were issued.

Great! So we can leave now, right?

"Not so fast," said the Indian government. India is a country that requires a visa to enter and exit. Once they became US citizens, the infants also became scofflaws: They were Americans in India without a visa. DJ and MJ needed to be granted exit visas from the Foreigner Regional Registration Office (FRRO) on their shiny new passports. The FRRO office in Mumbai is run by the Mumbai Police Department with the approval of an overseeing ministry in the capital of New Delhi.

Josh and I obtained tourist visas at the beginning of the international surrogacy process as directed by the agency we worked with. After we got to India and did the IVF procedure in November 2012, it was announced the next month that the visa guidelines for surrogacy had changed. Intended parents coming to India for the purposes of surrogacy were now required to travel on special medical visas, which were only issued to couples consisting of a man and woman married for at least two years. It was a not-so-subtle jab at gay intended parents seeking to have children through surrogacy.

Josh and I took solace in the fact that we had been "grandfathered in" before the new guidelines were publicized and enforced. However, we were also very sad and angry for the many gay intended parents who could have come after us, but now had that avenue closed to them for discriminatory reasons. We have since come to learn that many gay intended parents who had been looking to India are now directing their international surrogacy pursuits toward clinics in Thailand instead.

Even though we were "grandfathered in" before the new visa guidelines took effect, the process for getting exit visas from the FRRO had become more complicated. It used to be that these exit visas could be issued on the same day if you waited in line for a few hours. Now, we had to submit notarized documents proving we had started the surrogacy process before December 2012 and these documents needed to be reviewed by the main FRRO office in New Delhi before approval could be issued, possibly weeks later. Luckily, we made sure our paperwork did not raise any red flags and our agency had contacts who helped speed up the process.

Ultimately, about a month after the babies were born, the exit visas were issued and Josh returned triumphantly to the US, flying around the world alone with the little twins for a joyous family reunion. Pat was ready to start again immediately with the new twins and thus became possibly the world's most experienced twin nanny. JJ and AJ went back to school and had the most interesting summer vacation stories to tell their first-grade classmates.

Josh and I have since settled into a comfortable (if, at times, chaotic) routine, now juggling two sets of twins. We have found DJ and MJ to be much easier to handle, which we attribute to a combination of the babies being closer to full-term and Josh and I being more seasoned than your average parents of newborn twins. Whenever we go out as a family of six, we create a bit of a spectacle and attract curious glances from strangers trying to figure out exactly what is going on, but we are fortunate to have never had an unkind word spoken to us in public about being gay parents.

Whenever we get Josh's parents to babysit for a couple of hours so we can have a date night dinner out, Josh always starts the conversation by asking what our next big adventure will be. We are definitely done having children, but who knows where our next journey may lead?

# Kevin Wakelin

SAN FRANCISCO, CALIFORNIA

When I was a kid, I knew I wanted to have lots of children one day—or so my parents have often said. But truth be told, I actually do have vague memories of making such a declaration to my family on numerous occasions. I imagined a whole soccer team of kids with me as the doting dad. Fortunately, my folks never stood in the way of my unsubstantiated declarations, despite occasional dismissive eyeball rolls. My life has been one constant adventure of stepping out of the box, marching to my own beat and following my heart—maturing only by making every mistake there is to make. I've always loved kids, loved being a kid and still am a kid at heart.

By the time the real subject of whether or not to have children rolled around—back in 2000—there were many new opportunities for my then-partner and I to explore, including adoption and surrogacy. A number of trailblazers had already forged a path before us, but we definitely felt like a part of the new, emerging trend of visible alternative families.

Fortunately, we had done our fair share of footloose and fancy-free partying in our twenties. To be young, free, single and gay in San Francisco in the 1990s was hardly torturous. Throw in perfect synchronicity with the booming dot-com bubble around us and the fun times got even more interesting. With those days behind us, we happily sold our home in the heart of the Castro District and moved out to the East Bay suburbs into a spacious, single-family house with a yard, trees and room to grow—the perfect place to raise a family. There was no white picket fence but, within a year, I built one.

We had originally looked at adoption and went to many open house events for various agencies. Unfortunately, we were often the only gay couple in attendance. Many of the stories people shared revolved around infertility, which didn't apply to us, and the language used by the facilitators was not inclusive to same-sex couples. We asked about statistics on gay couples, but the answers we got back were always ambiguous. I know things have gotten better now, but back in the early 2000s, reaching out to same-sex couples was still a new thing for adoption agencies. So at the time, adoption just didn't seem like a good fit for us.

We changed course and began looking into gestational surrogacy, an expensive process involving an egg donor, a surrogate, our sperm, numerous doctors and many more attorneys. We ultimately found it to be the right choice for us, because it seemed like we could have more control over the process. We could be in charge of the timing, the people we interacted with and a lot of the genetics. The one thing that was left to Mother Nature was the sex of the child. Everything else was rather engineered. We decided to move forward with surrogacy, knowing that we had a better stake in the game.

Picking an egg donor was probably the hardest part. We were unprepared for the emotional and spiritual toll it took. We went through numerous binders to help make a selection. Did we want someone who was tall? Someone who was athletic? Someone who was smart? The process became uncomfortable for us and it started to feel like we were in a science-fiction movie. It was surreal trying to map out the genetic code of your biological child and we struggled with it.

Weeks went by and the selection process wasn't getting any easier, so we decided to start looking at donors in a different way. Instead of trying to choose someone based on medical history, SAT scores or genetic traits, we reviewed each profile and photo to determine who we could most likely be friends with based on hobbies, interests and cultural identities. The new method worked and in no time we had our donor!

Choosing a surrogate was a much smoother process. The agency pre-screens all applicants and the majority of them don't make it through that initial phase. Afterward, there is a matching service to help couples find a surrogate who fits in with their lifestyle choices. For example, some surrogates want to be left alone throughout the majority of their pregnancy, so they shouldn't be matched with a couple who wants a lot of contact. Some surrogates want communication after birth and others do not. We were lucky enough to match with a wonderful woman who lived close by.

The next step was for us to provide the sperm. We decided to mix ours together and have them battle it out to the finish line. This plan worked well for us, because throughout the whole process, from information gathering to the birth itself, we were completely engaged together without ever knowing which one of us actually fertilized the egg. It made for a sense of equality between us as a couple and was a powerful originator of equal bonding.

Because she lived so close to us, we had a lot of contact with our surrogate both before and after she became pregnant. It was wonderful for us, because we got to be involved with every medical appointment, from seeing the initial sonogram to hearing our child's first heartbeat. At the same time it was also a bit surreal, because here we were, thrust into an intimate relationship with a complete stranger.

We tried to do a lot of activities with our surrogate to normalize things. We went shopping, took hikes and had meals together. Sometimes she even stayed with us overnight. We wanted to establish a relationship with her now to ensure she stayed a part of our lives even after the baby was born. If our son or daughter ever had questions about where he or she came from, he or she could get real answers from people he or she knew.

With all the activities and doctor appointments going on, time flew by. At 3:00 A.M. some nine months later, we received a call that our surrogate's water had broken. We jumped into the car and drove to the hospital in Sacramento. We expected to get there quickly, since there was no traffic at that time in the morning, but weather in the Bay Area never cooperates. That night we drove twenty-five miles per hour on the highway in fog as thick as pea soup!

Luckily, we still arrived at the hospital in plenty of time. The staff working that night were great and well-prepared for a situation with a surrogate and two dads. You might think a birth is a birth, but that's not true. Every little thing counts and sometimes it's the littlest things that make the biggest impact. For example, there was a whiteboard in our room where the nurses wrote:

SURROGATE—OUR SURROGATE'S NAME
DADDY—MY PARTNER'S NAME
PAPA—KEVIN

Having this information in plain sight for everyone to see helped ensure the staff knew the appropriate language to use when coming into the room. That way a nurse didn't come in and ask our surrogate questions like "So, are you excited to be a mother?" There was no confusion on who the actual parents were and this made all the difference in the world.

Our hospital experience was amazing and when our daughter, Hana, was finally born, we were lucky enough to cut the cord. Then the baby was whisked away for cleaning and when the nurse brought her back, she handed our daughter to us first. Again, as a gay couple, it was nice to be recognized as the parents. We all spent the night in the hospital together where the staff had set up a room with three beds and a crib. The next morning, we left for home to begin the biggest chapter of our lives.

Hana was an incredibly contented baby. She slept through the night from three months on (I had created a spreadsheet of her eat-sleep-poop routine and posted it all over the house) and we seemed to be taking everything in stride. I worked a nine-to-five job while my partner stayed home tending to childcare. We're still in touch with our surrogate and have a great relationship with her. She comes to birthday parties, sends Christmas cards and sometimes goes on day trips with us.

One of the difficult parts about being a gay parent is that we constantly have to explain ourselves. Sometimes people will ask questions like "Whose is she?" as they try to find out who the biological father is—in their eyes, the "real" father. This is not an issue of being "his or his." We are both her parents. Language can have negative implications on children without us even knowing, so it's important to be mindful of the words we choose to say.

Our daughter started to have a lot of questions about our family when she was in second and third grade. Some of the kids at school asked why she didn't have a mom *and* a dad. We explained to her that she is very lucky, because she has two dads when many people don't. She also has an auntie (our surrogate), who helped carry her for her Daddy and Papa. She understands it and the other kids get it too when it's explained to them in an age-appropriate way. Kids are much smarter than many people give them credit for. When we chose an egg donor, we also checked a box that gives Hana the ability to contact her when she turns eighteen, if she chooses to do so. That way, if other complex questions surface later on down the road, she has a way of getting more detailed answers.

A few years after Hana was born, the relationship between my partner and I started to unravel. We were arguing, fighting and shouting all the time. We were no longer on the same page. Life was veering off track and alcohol was playing a lead role. After two more painful years, I decided the relationship was no longer salvageable. With a heavy heart, I moved out of that once-lovely family home and returned to the city, scratching my head and thinking, "Now what?"

Within a few months, Hana and I were back in the Castro District, living in a modest rented flat. I was now learning how to juggle the demands of being a single, working gay dad while also starting up a new real estate development venture in the worst recession of our times. Gone were the cars, the showcase house, the full-time nanny and the post-boom trappings. Hana's diabetes made the juggle even more challenging, as did negotiating an exit from my prior business partnership, which left me emotionally and financially drained. And somewhere in all of this mess was the realization that I was now a forty-year-old single working gay dad without a road map.

Fortunately, moving back to San Francisco was one of the better—if not the best—decisions I made. Living in the Castro District again reminded me that this community has always been full of trailblazers, constantly forging ahead into new, uncharted territories for a greater cause. Everyone seems to be on a mission, leading the way by example. And as I have discovered, I am not alone. Strollers and children are now a common, growing and important evolutionary thread in our gay community. However, it struck me that meeting other gay dads by happenstance wasn't going to produce many remarkable or reliable results.

In the spring of 2009, I created a social networking group called "Castro Dads." Within weeks, nearly a hundred dads had signed up. While online networking has its advantages, my goal was to create real community connections and relationships offline. So with the support of our openly gay District Supervisor Bevan Dufty and his daughter, Sidney, we reinvigorated an old tradition of a weekly drop-in gay dads dinner.

After a few short weeks, gay dads and their kids packed the restaurant, sharing stories, advice and support for each other. When Hana came up to me smiling at one of the dinners and said her new friend also had two gay, separated dads just like her, I could finally see my road map. As all the gay dads got to know each other and the kids too, I knew we were on our way to creating a connected and visible gay dads community. Watching this happen and helping nurture it along gives me the sort of joy that no working perk could ever do.

Somewhere between that bold, youthful declaration of having a soccer field full of kids and the reality of life kicking in, I have happily shed the fantasy of double-digit children and am instead raising one beautiful daughter, who turns six in January. Because I always saw myself having kids while also growing up cognizant of my sexual interest in men, I consider myself to be extremely lucky. I'm an openly gay man who had a child without denying my authentic sexual identity.

# PART 4
# ASSISTED REPRODUCTION

When lesbian couples decide to have children, it is very common for one person in the relationship to carry the baby. There are a few different ways that can be achieved:

1. A doctor can transfer a donor's sperm into a woman's uterus through a process called intrauterine insemination (IUI) so that natural fertilization can take place.

2. A woman can be inseminated through intracervical insemination (ICI), which is similar to IUI, except the sperm is placed near the cervix, rather than into the uterus. The cost of this procedure is typically much lower than IUI, since the sperm is placed farther away from the fallopian tubes.

3. A woman can be impregnated through a process known as in vitro fertilization (IVF), where the egg is fertilized prior to it being transferred into her uterus.

4. A woman can use the good ole do-it-yourself method. This doesn't mean that actual intercourse needs to happen, but there is always the "phone a friend" option where a male can help a female get pregnant without going to a doctor. Use your imagination.

There are many benefits that come with choosing assisted reproduction. Women in same-sex relationships can go through the experience of being pregnant together and support each other along the way. As a couple, they can participate in various things together including doctor visits, Lamaze classes and even birth.

If you choose to carry the baby, you will have full control when it comes to prenatal care. You can decide how many doctor visits you go to, how much exercise you get and whether or not to use prenatal vitamins and/or eat healthy organic foods. You can also refrain from using substances such as alcohol, drugs and tobacco that have been linked to birth defects.

Assisted reproduction gives you the benefit of being involved in your child's life from the moment he or she is conceived. You'll have the opportunity to see the baby's sonogram and even listen to your child's first heartbeat. If you are both in the same room during the actual delivery, your partner or spouse can support you by holding your hand, helping you with your breathing and comforting you along the way.

If you choose to move forward with assisted reproduction, you'll need to decide whether you want to use a known donor (for example, an acquaintance or friend) or an unknown donor. There are pros and cons in both scenarios.

When the donor is known, your child can develop a relationship with the donor as he or she grows up. Your child will have a better understanding of where he or she came from and why he or she might have certain characteristics and traits. However, there is a greater risk that the donor may later try to claim parental rights. There may even be a possibility that you or your partner could lose custody. When using a known donor, it is recommended that you consult with an attorney and have a Known Donor Agreement signed. Keep in mind that a Known Donor Agreement will not necessarily terminate the donor's rights, even if it says so. That's why consulting an attorney beforehand is crucial, especially since the laws vary by state.

If you choose an unknown donor through a sperm bank, you'll have access to the donor's comprehensive medical history and the ability to control your child's exposure to problematic genes. The specimens can also be quarantined and tested for sexually transmitted diseases. This can reduce the risk of passing anything on to you or your child. However, when using a sperm bank, the costs can add up depending on what services you select. Many insurance companies will not cover alternative insemination unless there is a diagnosis of "infertility" or if you have tried to inseminate without success for a period of time. Make sure you ask your health insurance company how they define infertility, what treatments are covered and if their policy covers insemination for same-sex couples.

One thing to keep in mind is that there is no guarantee that one of you will become pregnant after going through assisted reproduction treatments. You could wind up trying multiple times, which can become expensive. Costs can add up quickly. Also, cryobanks are not in every city, so you may not have a local clinic near you. This can make things a bit difficult when you have to arrange multiple doctor visits.

In this section of the book, you'll learn how a few women who were in same-sex relationships chose to get pregnant through assisted reproduction. Some of the couples enlisted their male friends to help them. They explain how the eggs were fertilized at home without having sex and how many times their male friends actually had to make donations. Their experiences are completely different from those who sought the help of fertility clinics.

Along the way, you'll hear how some women dealt with various unexpected occurrences, like the the devastation of having a miscarriage and being treated differently at the hospital during birth.

# Elaine Boyd and Cathy Smith

It was an ordinary Tuesday night, except we were sitting around a dining table with friends, laughing our asses off over a game of Pictionary. Oh... *and* I was waiting for a sperm delivery from our friend Dave.

Our game was full-tilt when I saw the clock and realized Dave was going to knock at the door any minute, delivery in hand. Even the most self-assured man in the world most likely didn't want to face the knowing smiles of four women at such a moment. We needed to wrap our game up quickly. Our friends could not get enough of the scene. "Oh darn it, now where did I leave my keys? It will take *at least* twenty minutes to find them! Wait, wait...How about if *we* answer the door and tell him it's the wrong house?"

It wasn't your everyday scenario.

How did we get here? It starts with my partner, now spouse, Cathy. She resisted the idea at first. We were reading quietly in bed one evening, six months into our relationship, when I casually mentioned I'd always wanted a kid. Cathy looked surprised, fixed her eyes on my face and asked if I was serious—I was. Her reaction suggested that Cathy and I were miles apart on that issue—we were.

Given that response, I was surprised when Cathy e-mailed me several website links on "pregnancy after thirty-five" the next day. Maybe she could warm up to this idea?

Cathy and I had the beginnings of a good relationship. She is smart, compassionate, sane, super-cute and very considerate. She's also quiet; I'm chatty. We shared a love of international travel and other cultures and had similar tastes and values in general. We enjoyed each other's company, but are two very independent people and had no plans of moving in together. In any case, our future together looked promising.

I'm from a big family and always wanted a kid. On my thirty-ninth birthday, a friend from Los Angeles called and asked, "Elaine, are you still thinking of having a child?" I said yes and she said, "What are you waiting for? You are thirty-nine years old!"

Those old-worlders don't mince words and those were the words that prompted me to float the idea with Cathy. And to eventually talk to Dave.

"Do you want to have a kid together?" That's a question I've gotten twice over the years, from two different male friends. Both of the lovely gentlemen who asked me about it were smart and handsome. Both were also blonde and fair-skinned like me, a deal-breaker. Growing up in sunny San Diego, a bit of skin-saving melanin is a good thing.

The biological father of my child had to be someone who didn't pink up like a British tourist after ten minutes of sun. I needed a touch of swarthy. My old buddy Dave leapt to mind. Yes, Dave might be a good one to ask. Smart and funny? Check! Relaxed and good-natured? Check! Winning smile and fun to hang out with? Check and check. Also, I knew that if anything ever went sideways between us, we'd sit down and talk like civilized people, without involving legal dogs.

I called Dave after my thirty-ninth birthday lecture and asked him. We talked about what the situation might look like. We decided for Dave not to have any custody during childhood, but he could see this kid whenever he liked. We eventually had a legal agreement drawn up that essentially said he couldn't ask me for custody and I couldn't ask him for money.

He was on board—an accomplice! Two years later, we actually got busy. His end of the bargain was to provide genetic material, delivered to my house in a container. At that time, Dave was not in a relationship, which was unusual for him. We laughed about how the one time he wasn't "getting lucky" was when he might father a child.

*The Essential Guide to Lesbian Conception, Pregnancy and Birth* promised me that sperm could live for thirty minutes outside the body, as long as it was kept at body temperature. It also said that the receptacle didn't have to be sterile, just clean and dry. How about an empty baby food jar? That worked.

Figuring out my fertile days was daunting. I knew straight couples who "coupled" every day for a full two weeks around ovulation time and still didn't get pregnant. How the hell were we going to get it right with just one or two shots a month?

Everyone and their mother had a different way to know when you're fertile. One of my sisters had twice conceived near the last day of her period, so that gave me a rough idea of when I was likely to be fertile, too.

For more specific timing, we turned to something called an Ovulite. It's an internally-lit magnifying glass, the size of a lipstick. You put your morning saliva on the glass slide and if you're fertile, there is a "ferning" pattern. Yes, like a garden fern.

Most of the time your spit just looks like magnified pond scum on the Ovulite. But sure enough, occasionally my saliva showed the ferning pattern on the glass. On the days I got the pattern, Cathy checked it out too to verify I wasn't seeing things and then I called Dave.

"Hello, Dave? Yeah, hi. Um, I think today is a good day. Did you get the baby food jars? Can you, um…Would today work out for you?" Dave was as good as his word and said he'd try to make it happen. He got baby food jars too (he figured bananas were an appropriate selection).

Dave showed up at my door with the delivery. Cathy was elsewhere in the house, so I greeted him alone. It was equally weird for both of us, that first time he handed over the body-temperature genetic material. But by the second time, the novelty sort of wore off. We both had the end goal in mind.

One of my sisters, a registered nurse up in the Central Valley, sent me an assortment of plastic syringes for the basting effort. The conception guide tells you to lie on your back with a pillow elevating your pelvis, suction the sperm from the jar into the syringe, then insert the syringe and squeeze. You stay that way for about twenty minutes. After that, you're supposed to lie on each side for ten minutes.

As you can see, it was a low-tech operation. No doctors, no hospitals, no frozen or "cleaned" sperm, just a glass jar and a plastic syringe.

One afternoon, after our sixth attempt, I threw my car in reverse while backing out of a parking spot. Twisting back to look behind me, I noticed some breast tenderness—a famous sign of possible pregnancy. It surprised me a little, but I told myself I was just imagining it. Still, I decided to go get a pregnancy test to be sure. I went to the store, grabbed a generic pregnancy test and dashed to the checkout, feeling a little jittery.

It was the only thing I bought, so there it sat on the conveyer belt, its cheap black-and-white packaging screaming PREGNANCY TEST in large, bold letters, a solitary item with separator bars on either side. My wandering mind took no immediate note of it. Then a pang of self-consciousness hit me when I realized what I was advertising to the people around me in the crowded checkout line—this was way worse than a single-item tampon purchase. If I'd had my wits about me I'd have nabbed a loaf of bread to lay strategically on top of the PREGNANCY TEST. I tried to look nonchalant.

I got home, unwrapped the stick and looked at the directions: "Urinate directly onto stick." I did that and nothing. I felt a mixture of both relief and disappointment.

While reading further over all the directions, I noticed this additional instruction: "Wait at least three minutes for results." Had I waited three minutes before tossing the stick? I thought I had, but decided to take another look to be sure. I reached down and retrieved the stick from the small bathroom wastebasket. It now had a large, unmistakable pink plus-sign on it, a positive result. I nearly fainted.

My very first reaction was, "Oh, shit, what have I done?" I called Cathy on her cell phone immediately. "I'm pregnant," I told her. "I thought I wasn't, but it was there. In the trash. The plus sign. On the stick. I didn't see it at first. It was there, the pink plus sign. I'm freaking pregnant!"

Cathy, ever the picture of calmness, replied, "Oh my God. I'm driving right now, but I need to pull over. Oh my God, I'm gonna pull over."

Frankly, we were both in shock. I'm not sure how much either of us believed this could work, despite assurances to the contrary. A friend's brother, a cardiologist, was convinced that getting pregnant this way was not possible and to this day he's absolutely certain we did it the old fashioned way. But he was wrong—it worked! After the shock wore off, Cathy and I were excited.

As a forty-one-year-old, newly-pregnant woman, the specter of miscarriage darkened my thoughts from the very beginning. I'm not usually superstitious, but I didn't even sneak peeks at baby clothes for the first six months of my pregnancy.

Unbeknownst to us, a distant family member got very early word of our news and immediately sent infant booties in the mail. Not suspecting a thing, I opened the package and got spooked by those insidious frilly things, my kryptonite. I dashed to the other side of the room and hollered at Cathy, "Oh, holy crap, close that box!" We ditched the box in the deepest recesses of the hall closet where its evil juju was less potent.

Little did we suspect, but my baby bump precipitated an avalanche of gifts and a huge outpouring of love, support and well-wishing. A baby on the way was a great equalizer. Queer or not, people get behind a pregnant couple.

We were grateful for the support, too, because we needed it. A friend threw us a beautiful baby shower and suggested we do a registry. We visited a local store, walked inside and froze in place over the vast and bewildering consumer circus in front of us. There were miles and miles of baby stuff. Lactation accoutrements alone occupied what seemed like a full city block. How on earth could you know what you'd need?

We probably needed a stroller, but what kind? What was better, a swinging chair or a vibrating chair? Or should we ditch them both for a jumper? Was there a trick to picking out the exact right crib, mattress or changing table? Did we need a nursing pillow, a baby intercom or special laundry soap? And for the love of God, someone please tell us if there is any damn difference between leading diaper brands!

Fortunately, our family and friends helped us navigate this new universe. Their support carried us through. Not everyone was initially supportive, though. Early on in the process, I checked in with my doctor, looking for feedback on my age and any general getting-pregnant-after-forty advice. As I described our plan to her, I started to realize she was mentally checking out on me. To this day, I hold an indelible image of her standing in front of me in her white doc-smock, arms folded across her chest, a little gold cross pendent glinting under the fluorescent light and shaking her head, saying, "I don't think this is going to work."

She was wrong, too. It did work. I was absolutely, positively pregnant. It was a difficult pregnancy, because I had morning, noon and night sickness every day, the entire time. I had the classic sensitivity to smells, perfumes especially. I could detect a scented candle from ten or twelve feet away. My only odd craving was for olive oil. Even though my taste buds were completely screwed up for the whole pregnancy, I wanted crusty French bread just so I could soak it in olive oil.

Cathy and I are not heavy drinkers, but we are routine drinkers, so being dry for nine months was rough! I probably would have sneaked a glass of wine here or there during the pregnancy, but Cathy had read too much on Fetal Alcohol Syndrome and made me promise not to.

On August 10, 2006, our daughter, Claire, came into the world. She was 6 pounds, 11 ounces and had a mass of black hair. Cathy and Dave were both in the room. There were a few complications toward the end, but everything turned out fine. I was so excited to see the face of this little baby who had been moving around inside of me all that time.

I've heard people say they felt an immediate love for their newborns. I felt something more akin to animalistic mama-bear protectiveness. I recall arriving back home after my two-day hospital stay and seeing our brand new next-door neighbors standing in the front yard when we pulled up. We hadn't met them yet and I had this weird instinct not to let them see we had this new baby. I'm not sure I can say why I felt that way. In retrospect, it was irrationally protective, but animal instincts aren't always rational.

Little Claire was so soft, tiny and warm. Holding her and nursing her brought a feeling that words don't quite capture. Like that surge of emotion you feel when hearing beautiful music, you feel it in your body: a oneness, a warm sensation. It feels primal.

There is also the lack-of-sleep part. That part is less fun. Sometimes I felt so sleep-deprived that I seriously worried about my ability to care for my baby, but it worked out fine.

People sometimes ask if I had postpartum depression. After feeling seasick for nine months straight, I had postpartum elation! It was great to feel good again. I vividly recall my first meal right after giving birth—it was an iceberg lettuce salad with a squeeze packet of ranch dressing, a soft, white roll and (gag) margarine. Any other day of my life I'd have turned my nose up at that meal, but at that moment, it was glorious manna from above. I could taste food again!

In the delivery room as Claire came out, I called for a gin and tonic. I actually got a beer instead. That was glorious, too.

When it came down to filling out the birth certificate, we originally wanted Dave listed as the father for genealogical purposes; however, we were told that when Cathy legally adopted Claire down the road, a new birth certificate was going to be issued with Cathy's name taking Dave's place, so we didn't add him. To our surprise, we were able to have both Cathy's name and mine on the original certificate with no issues whatsoever.

Our little girl is now seven years old and a real force of nature. Every week, every month is a new installment of watching her development. First it was walking, then talking. She said her first word at sixteen months during Christmastime. We had just decorated the tree with lights. Cathy turned it on and the whole tree lit up in twinkling colors and Claire let out a long, drawn-out "Wow!" We cracked up.

Those first couple of years as we bathed her or changed her diapers, it struck me again and again how overwhelmingly vulnerable little human children are. They rely on us completely. It made me want to enact legislation requiring all people to take psychological profile exams before they could procreate. Sometimes I feel gay parents really are best because such an effort precedes parenthood.

Cathy and I live happily with our daughter here in San Diego and have never regretted our decision to have a kid. We live on a block with several other children her age and they all hang out a lot. We love our little girl and are grateful to Dave. His whole family adores Claire and his mother faithfully remembers her every birthday and Christmas.

Early on, we talked about Dave's dating life and whether it was going to be weird for him to tell a potential mate that he'd helped someone get pregnant. I loved his answer: "The most important thing in a relationship is understanding. If a potential mate can't fathom why I wanted to do this, then they're not the right person for me." He eventually found the right person and they are now married. Claire has been treated with nothing but love and kindness from the two of them and she adores them both.

We are an extended, untraditional family. Our families have all come together with great adoration for Claire. She is a true delight and Cathy and I are both so glad that we didn't miss out on being parents.

# Sarah Ann Gilbert

### DENVER, COLORADO

Wanting a second child as gay parents was a bit like playing the lottery a second time and assuming we had a better chance of winning. It was easy to believe that the odds of us having another baby were one in four: We had four frozen embryos and we wanted one child.

But statistics don't care what you believe.

My initial round of fertility treatments resulted in seven fertilized eggs. But then we lost one of them. After that, we lost a fetus at around eight weeks. The fetus "failed to develop," as the doctor told us on a cold November day, as though she were describing a change in the weather. "Most women don't even know that they're pregnant when it happens," she said.

And then our daughter, Wynn, was born healthy and alive.

This happened all at once, because that is the other rule of the game. You tend to get nothing or everything—triplets, for example. When you are going through in vitro fertilization, you must use your embryos two or three at a time. It increases your odds of having a baby.

We had used up three zygotes and I had given birth to one baby in just one round of treatment. And even though we really wanted to have just one more baby, we might end up with three. But three seemed so much better than none.

We bought our tickets.

"Is there anything we need to do before using the frozen eggs we have in storage?" I asked the nurse.

"No," she said. "You'll just need to have them transferred to our lab where they'll be thawed. And then an embryologist will determine how many of the embryos are viable."

"Really?" I was astonished by the simplicity of it all. "I don't need to take any drugs?" It occurred to me that I might sound like an addict at that moment. But these weren't the kind of drugs you do for fun unless experiencing the combined symptoms of PMS, menopause and pregnancy is your idea of a good time.

"No drugs," said the nurse, who was dressed casually in a golf shirt and jeans. I didn't believe her. Maybe she wasn't actually a nurse. Or maybe she was just forgetting something. Surely there would be pain-killers, at least.

"I'm still breastfeeding. Does that matter?" I asked.

"That's okay," she said. "You might want to stop, but it shouldn't matter."

I was a bit disappointed by her answer. I was looking for a reason to stop. Breastfeeding wasn't that fun. Production was down and there had been enough industrial spills with the breast pump in my office that the place might start to stink. Besides, our daughter had started eating solid food now, so she didn't *need* breast milk anymore, did she?

"How old is she?" asked the nurse, looking down at Wynn, who was on the floor in her car seat.

"Eight months."

"Wow, she's a big girl."

*So am I*, I thought. We were both in the ninety-fifth percentile for height. And while I held myself accountable for a lot of her height, I blamed our sperm donor for all the future conversations about women's basketball that she will have to endure. It wasn't my fault that finding a short sperm donor was harder than finding an ugly supermodel.

"This guy looks good," my spouse said while clicking through the thousands of donors available in the online database for a popular cryo-bank. "Oh never mind. He's six-foot-three," she added, returning to the search page.

"You should screen for people who are short," I often told her. "Try looking for people who are five-foot-nine."

"There aren't any," she replied.

I didn't have the patience to go through donor profiles one by one, so I came up with ways to narrow down the search. This is how we decided that we wanted a short donor with green eyes. I have green eyes, so that increased the chances of our baby looking like me. And green eyes are rare, so that would narrow the search. Eventually, we found our donor. He was five-foot-nine with green eyes, which doesn't really explain why our daughter was born with brown eyes.

But as soon as Wynn was born, I knew I wanted to have another baby. I liked being a parent a lot more than I had imagined. My friends, like me, were surprised by my unforeseen tenderness toward our daughter. I loved her more every day.

But there was another reason I wanted Wynn to have a sibling, a reason I only told myself in the middle of the night when I woke up with anxiety about how her life might be. I worried about her feeling lonely and socially isolated as the only child of gay, older parents. And I felt guilty about it, because I knew what it felt like to be left out.

Now I worried that my daughter might feel the same way. Would she learn to listen and watch as carefully as I did to determine if someone was homophobic before telling them about her moms? Or before she asked her friends to come over to play after school? Would she be gay by extension? If the answer was going to be "yes," then I thought I could at least give her someone to share the misery with, someone related to her and even someone who was part of the same batch.

Choosing to start our family using the mainstream medical system felt like the most comfortable choice for us. We liked the idea that everything was scientific and federally regulated, that there were going to be a lot of experts guiding us throughout the process and protecting our health and our rights along the way. Perhaps we were being optimistic and naïve, but in some ways that gave us the endurance that we would need for our journey.

The physical battles in fertility treatments are fought and won in two-week increments between ovulation and menstruation. But the war against self-doubt and hopelessness doesn't have a timeline. So when we found out that all I needed to do to have a second child was show up on the right day and hope for the best, I was so relieved that I wanted to have the baby immediately.

The first step was getting the fertilized eggs.

I called the clinic and asked what was needed to transfer the fertilized eggs from the lab to our doctor's office. "Some paperwork and a method of transport," said the nurse on the other end of the phone. The eggs could be shipped through the mail or I could come and get them. This was our first family carpool.

I chose Memorial Day to drive to the clinic and retrieve our four frozen embryos. As I got out of the car, a slight breeze whispered below the cloudless, blue sky. There was no one around, which made me feel more, instead of less, self-conscious about driving around on a holiday weekend, tending to my own medical procedures. In just a few minutes, I was going to have human embryos in my possession, so I half-expected pro-lifers to jump out of the bushes and rush at me with accusatory questions.

I walked into the clinic, explained to the woman at the front desk why I was there and she called the lab. Then I sat in the waiting area across from a couple—a man and a woman. It had been more than a year since I was there, but everything looked the same. Blonde-haired, blue-eyed babies on brochures stared at me with their placid faces, willing me to store my cord blood or try some drug I couldn't pronounce.

A lab technician appeared from a back room wheeling a dolly that carried a surprisingly large, hard plastic canister shaped like a fat dart and covered in stickers that shouted OVERNIGHT and FRAGILE. I had expected to see something smaller and more sterile looking.

Together, the technician and I wheeled it out to my car and put it in the front seat. Being approximately the size of a human torso without arms or legs, it fit perfectly. And just to make sure it wouldn't be killed in an accident, I put its seatbelt on. I thanked the technician profusely, took one more paranoid look around for pro-lifers and sat myself down in the driver's seat.

Now it was just the two of us. *Actually, the five of us*, I thought, glancing over at the canister. It felt like I was on a date. It was just a plastic container, but together, we were driving away from all the hardship of the fertility treatments and into a hopeful future of sisters or brothers for the child I already loved so much. My sense of freedom and contentment was palpable.

I quietly hoped our next child was a girl. Not because I didn't want a boy. I have nothing against boys. It simply seemed perfect to imagine Wynn having a sister. Sisters fought over jeans and made up over shared secrets. Sisters called each other on Saturdays when they couldn't decide what movie to see or had their hearts broken. Sisters were bound by immutable laws of bonding, friendship and blood. I wanted that for my daughter.

"This way," said the nurse as she showed me back to a large exam room furnished with the requisite paper-covered table and laminate-faced countertops and cupboards. Unlike the other rooms I had been in, this one contained a large, flat-screen TV mounted on the wall. Maybe there was a game on and no one wanted to miss it. Or possibly an advertiser had sponsored it.

I glanced at the TV. The screen showed two large, watery orbs that looked like clusters of soap bubbles. They were floating around, but also looked busy and even frustrated. I stared more closely. I could see new bubbles being created inside and sometimes outside each of the orbs.

"This one is hatching," said the doctor gleefully, pointing to one of the fertilized eggs on the screen.

Those were my eggs. There were two of them.

The only thing I could think to say was, "You call it hatching? That's adorable."

"Yes. And it's a really good sign. You see this area, the dark part? That is where the baby is starting to form," the doctor explained.

There was a dark cluster of smaller cells in one corner of one of the bubbles. I felt like I could see the cells dividing or at least getting organized to form something important, like a leg or a head. This is what hope must look like, I thought.

"You can have the video," said the doctor.

I laughed. Some people make videos of their child's first steps, a clip of their first turn on the ski slopes or their first rollercoaster ride at

Disneyland. Our family was getting a video of our child's first cells dividing. My parents would be proud.

The two viable eggs were inserted effortlessly in my uterus. Then I went home to wait. I was scheduled to go back to the clinic in ten days for a blood test to determine if I was pregnant, followed by an ultrasound. If there was a baby, the ultrasound would show a tiny blinking light in an enormous black chasm. I had seen it before. The blinking light was the baby's heart cells and on the monitor you could see them beat, flashing on and off like a miniature lighthouse.

If there was a heartbeat, that meant more appointments and more ultrasounds to track the baby's progress until I could be released from the fertility clinic fish tank and into the vast ocean of regular pregnant women getting prenatal care.

I felt sick. I hoped that it was morning sickness, but I had never had morning sickness before, so I might have just been sick with worry. I tried to relax. I wasn't forty yet. There was still time to have more babies if we really, really, really wanted them.

The days passed and I went to the lab for the test. The nurses were kind and hopeful. They were also encouraging. And the next day, in the middle of a sunny Colorado afternoon, my cell phone rang. I stepped outside and sat down at a picnic table to answer it. I thought I might pass out.

"This is Sarah."

"You're pregnant," said the nurse. She said some other stuff first, like her name, but I didn't hear it.

"I'm so glad," I said, the sense of relief noticeable in my voice. "Because I feel terrible. And if I'm not pregnant, I need to go to the hospital to see what's wrong with my stomach."

She laughed and said, "We need to make an appointment for you to come in for an ultrasound, so we can see what's in there."

"Well, I hope it's either a baby or thirty thousand dollars," I said, because I didn't really want anything else.

A few days later, my spouse and I went with Wynn, still in her car seat, to the clinic. I sat uncomfortably in a hospital gown on the paper-covered table. The nurse put the ultrasound wand in the correct and very personal spot from which we could see my uterus.

There was a single blinking light. The last viable egg from a batch of seven had implanted and was growing and winking at us.

We all stared at it.

That blinking light was Wynn's sister.

She was born in March and we named her Marlo.

We had won the lottery.

Again.

# Rudene and Anna-Marie du Preez

PRETORIA, SOUTH AFRICA

Our journey started in 2004, when Anna-Marie and I met on a local dating site. I was seventeen then and Anna-Marie had just turned twenty-one. We communicated for three months before meeting for the first time. We had an instant connection and could talk for hours on the phone and face-to-face. I told Anna-Marie from the start that I loved children and wanted kids of my own one day. It was my life's dream. We moved in together in early 2005 and also got engaged, even though gay marriage was not legal here in South Africa. However, that all changed in 2006 when the Civil Union bill was passed in our country.

The same year I moved in with Anna-Marie, I also met someone who had gone through artificial insemination. Her son was already four years old. Before that, having children of our own was only a dream and seemed like a very expensive and improbable prospect for us. I became good friends with this woman and received a lot of information about the process and its legal aspects.

Anna-Marie and I got married in August 2008. As a young married couple, we enjoyed travelling South Africa and taking regular vacations together. We were always a low-key couple, enjoying jobs in and around the house. We also did not really care for going to clubs or pubs. We preferred having friends over to our home for a barbeque or dinner party.

Towards the latter half of 2009, we met more gay and lesbian couples with children and gathered even more information—specifically speaking with teenage children of the couples to hear what their challenges were in school and how they felt about having an "alternative" family. After gaining this perspective, Anna-Marie and I started talking about having children of our own. We continued investigating how to do the insemination ourselves. We felt it was a more comfortable and relaxed setting than a doctor's office. It also meant that we could both be actively involved in the process.

So we started tracking my menstrual cycle in October of 2009 to get an indication of how long my cycle was and where in my cycle I was ovulating. I was luckily regular and we pinpointed that my ovulation took place on my CD (cycle day) 18 and 19.

We kept monitoring my cycle and in January 2010 I contacted a cryobank to get donor information and to find out if they could ship the sperm to us. They gave us the contact details for a laboratory in Pretoria. It wasn't too far from where we lived, so I contacted the laboratory and scheduled a consultation. Anna-Marie couldn't get any leave from work, so I went on my own.

The woman I consulted with assumed I was heterosexual. She made condescending remarks about homosexual couples who had come in for consultations in the past. I immediately started acting more straight. The lady asked questions about my "husband." What colour hair did he have? What colour eyes? How tall was he? What kind of career did he have? What hobbies did he enjoy? I gave her Anna-Marie's descriptions as my answers. Then the consultant gave me the number of the donor she thought most fit my description. As I was leaving, she asked me to please bring my husband with me the next day to confirm the donor profile was a fit.

I was so gobsmacked that I didn't know what to do. We wanted a child, but now here was this obstacle. I thought that it might be best to find someone who could act as my husband, just so we could get the sperm. I got into my car and phoned three of our male friends, asking each of them to be my fake husband. All of them said they didn't mind helping out. The third one asked why we were using a sperm bank and why we didn't just ask him to donate. We had a long discussion with him, especially about the involvement and rights of the donor. He agreed that this was a gift from him to us and that he didn't want to be involved in the child's life. We had a donor contract drawn up with an attorney while we were still doing our research.

On February 18, 2010, I tested positive for ovulation, so we phoned our friend and asked him to make the first donation for us. He came to our house, made his donation and then left. We had the apparatus ready and did the insemination ourselves. It was very funny—Anna-Marie was so nervous that she shook the whole time and spilled some of the sperm. She tried re-inserting it a couple of times. After the insemination, I was lying on the bed, feet and bum in the air, thinking "What if we did it wrong?"

We performed another insemination the next day. After the two-week waiting period, I took a pregnancy test. It was negative, but this was still a couple of days before the start of my menstruation, so I waited two more days and did another test. Once again, it showed negative. It was now the day before I was due to start menstruation. I waited another couple of days and tested once more. Initially the test showed negative.

My sister's son was visiting us that afternoon and noticed the test stick on the counter and asked what it was. I explained it to him and then he asked what it meant if there were two stripes. I told him that one stripe meant "not pregnant" and two stripes meant "pregnant." He got all excited and congratulated me on being pregnant, but I told him that the test had shown negative after the indicated waiting period and that it was probably just a false positive.

The second stripe made me a bit excited, but also very uncertain. So I decided to take another pregnancy test and this time it showed a positive right away. We then went for a blood test, just to confirm I was indeed pregnant. The blood test also had a positive result and determined that I was already about five weeks pregnant. I then started searching for a gay-friendly gynecologist, which turned out to be a mission as well. But our very first sonar was an amazing experience and hearing our baby's first heartbeat brought tears to my eyes. How lucky can a person get? Anna-Marie and I spoke to so many people who had tried to conceive for years with no luck. We both believed we had been given the most incredible gift ever. It was the gift of new life, but little did we know just how much this gift was going to change our own lives.

At nine weeks, I had bad morning sickness and the only food I could keep in was basmati rice. My queasiness lasted throughout the day and drained my energy. I felt okay in the evenings, though, and could enjoy a good night's rest.

We started early with buying nappies, wipes and clothes and getting the baby's room ready. We did everything ourselves: We painted all the walls of our house, took out the carpets and installed laminated floors. I remember we did one room when I was four months pregnant and I could help without getting tired or uncomfortable. But when we started on the next room, I was five months along and struggled with the task, because my tummy had grown quite a lot and was now getting in the way. We bought all of the big things like the stroller, car seat, feeding chair, camping cot and a compactum [changing table] by the time I was five months pregnant. We were two hens getting the nest ready for our little chick.

At twenty-one weeks, I changed to a different gynecologist. The one I had been seeing wanted to put me on medication I was allergic to. I was scared that while I was in labour, she might give me medication that caused adverse effects. Later on in our prenatal classes, I heard others say that this gynecologist tended to forget things very easily.

When I moved to the new gynecologist, we found out that our miracle baby was a little boy. My family thought I was having a girl, so I had dreams of playing with dolls and having tea parties with our daughter. When the gynecologist told us it was actually a boy, I had to rebuild the puzzle. There and then, I realised this was how heterosexual parents must feel when their gay children come out of the closet.

So the hunt began for a boy's name. Anna-Marie and I wanted something English that was a combination of both names and had a beautiful meaning. We spent a whole day searching and looking at names. In the end, we decided on Aden ("A" from Anna-Marie and "den" from Rudene). Aden also means Little Fire. We also picked Declan as a second name, which means "full of goodness."

Our little boy was born in November 2010, by way of a C-section at thirty-nine weeks and one day. I was not very emotional due to the calming medication they gave me before the caesarean, but Anna-Marie was booming with pride and had the biggest smile on her face. After we were moved into our hospital room, a lactation nurse came and assisted us with the baby's latching. He latched like a professional and drank for twenty minutes until the nurses came around to help me clean. While the nurses were busy with me, Anna-Marie held Aden in her arms and he started sucking his little hand. It was such a special moment and very encouraging to see how strong his sucking reflex was.

Right after the C-section, I wanted to stand up and change his nappy, but I had to lie down the whole day. That was very difficult for me, but Anna-Marie was an amazing mother. She stepped in and changed nappies, bathed Aden and even helped him to latch correctly onto my breast. This little person was completely dependent on us for everything. Feed him, bathe him and burp him—love and care for him.

We were discharged two days after Aden's birth. On day three, we went to see the pediatrician, who told us the baby had jaundice. I remember standing in the hospital holding him and realising that we were responsible for his well-being. I felt helpless. Anna-Marie told me not to worry, that she was going to sort this out, and she did. We got a blue-light bed for Aden and a nurse to come check on him every day. It was a difficult time. We could hardly hold him, because he had to be on the blue light as much as possible to cure the jaundice. Luckily, we could do this at home and did not have to leave him in the hospital.

Aden was very happy breastfeeding. He did not want to suck on a bottle. He was a real mommy's boy and didn't like strangers. It was amazing to see how this little person grew and developed almost every day.

Aden changed our lives completely; his presence changed our way of thinking. He motivates us to do things differently and knowing he is here gives us hope each and every morning. Sometimes it feels like he was at our wedding day or that he was there when we first met each other.

A few months after Aden was born, Anna-Marie had a project with a client in Cape Town and we went along with her. Aden flew on a plane at a very young age. He got to feel sea sand before he was six months old. He loved being outside and he liked animals. He touched a black Rhino calf when he was seven months old and had a close encounter with a lion when he was eleven months old.

We were building so many new memories with our little boy and couldn't imagine our lives without him. By the time Aden turned one, we started discussing having another child, but decided to wait and enjoy our time alone with him a bit longer first. We wanted to spend as much time as possible with him. He was our pride and joy.

Before Aden turned two, we decided to start trying for our second child. Anna-Marie wanted to get pregnant this time around. That posed a new challenge for us, because Anna-Marie's period was irregular, which meant she had to use fertility drugs.

We consulted with our doctor, who prescribed medication for Anna-Marie over a three-month period. She started taking it in November, just after Aden's second birthday. It was a difficult time, because the medication caused Anna-Marie to experience hot flashes and terrible mood swings. It did, however, help to get her cycle regular. We inseminated in November, December and January without any success. Before we inseminated in February, we went to a gynecologist to see if anything was wrong. On the sonar, the doctor could see three eggs that were ready to be released from Anna-Marie's ovary.

We were very excited and proceeded to inseminate for seven consecutive days, the most we've ever done. Two weeks later, Anna-Marie tested herself and two of the tests showed a positive result. We went for a blood test about a week later, but this showed a negative result and Anna-Marie started menstruating two days afterwards. We were shattered. Anna-Marie had what's known as a chemical pregnancy, a very early miscarriage. She bled profusely for seven days.

After the chemical pregnancy, we decided to discontinue the fertility treatment for Anna-Marie. Then I stopped breastfeeding completely and we inseminated me in March, April, May and June. In early July 2012, I got a positive pregnancy test. We were once again excited, but a couple of days later I started with my period, which meant I also had an early miscarriage. Once again, we were shaken to our cores and decided not to inseminate again.

The next couple of months were very difficult for us, as we worked through the miscarriages. I got depressed after I stopped breastfeeding and felt I was no longer needed by Aden. Anna-Marie also had a lot of work stress, which made things more challenging.

By October, we had worked through these trials and found things slowly getting back to normal. We talked about trying again. Anna-Marie ovulated on October 28th, but we couldn't find a donor.

On November 4th, I tested to see if I was ovulating and got a positive result. I called our donor, who said he was available and willing to donate. He made the donation and, as I was putting it into a syringe, I decided that we should both inseminate. I proceeded to split the sperm into two syringes and told Anna-Marie to lie down. I inseminated her and she inseminated me. The next day I tested positive for ovulation again and Anna-Marie inseminated me, but she didn't want to split the sperm this time, because she was scared of not getting pregnant and wasting the sperm.

Twelve days later, Anna-Marie tested and got a faint second line on her pregnancy test. However, we didn't want to get too excited, given our previous experiences. Two days later, Anna-Marie woke up with a terrible neck spasm and went to our general practitioner. The doctor wanted to send Anna-Marie for X-rays, but we told him that we suspected she might be pregnant. He performed a test right there in his office and it also showed positive. We couldn't believe our eyes. I sat for hours, staring at the test, thinking this baby was a miracle. One thing I learned from all the difficult moments is that if the time is right, it will happen. No matter what you do or how hard you try to do things "right," it will work out the way it was meant to work out.

Anna-Marie's pregnancy was very uneventful. She did not experience any morning sickness or have many complaints or cravings. However, she did have some back pain the last couple of weeks leading up to her due date.

Anna-Marie woke up around 2:30 A.M. on the morning of the 28th, feeling that she had to go to the bathroom. She went, but nothing happened and then the feeling went away. She got back in bed, but the feeling returned a few minutes later. She got up a second time, but the same thing occurred. She started to suspect that she might be in labour. When it happened the third time, Anna-Marie woke me and we started monitoring the contractions. She was certainly in labour, but the contractions were very irregular. We contacted our midwife and she advised that Anna-Marie should sit in a lukewarm bath for at least thirty to forty-five minutes while we kept monitoring the contractions.

About forty-five minutes later, we called the midwife again with our results. The contractions were now more regular and about four to five minutes apart. The midwife advised Anna-Marie to stay in the bath for another thirty minutes and then try to get some sleep. Anna-Marie attempted to go to sleep, but the contractions had gotten closer together and they were lasting longer. She walked around the house and used the coping methods we had learned in our prenatal classes to get through each contraction.

By 6:00 A.M., Anna-Marie was really struggling with the pain as the contractions were even closer together. Our midwife had not yet come to our home to inspect how far Anna-Marie was dilated, because she was called to assist another mother who had been in labour for two days already.

At 6:30 A.M., Anna-Marie told me to pack everything in the car. The midwife contacted me and said she believed Anna-Marie was further than everyone had thought. I phoned our mothers so they could also be part of the birth experience.

I stayed calm and realised I had to get Aden to my father, who was going to look after him while we were busy with the birth. I left Anna-Marie in the bath at home and rushed out with Aden. Then I returned as fast as I could and helped Anna-Marie out of the bath. We started to walk to the car and as we were about to exit the house, Anna-Marie had another contraction. We stopped and she told me to feel. I put my hand against her pants and felt the head.

That was when I realised our daughter was coming and coming fast. We arrived at the birth house and the midwife started with the regular exam. Anna-Marie was fully dilated and needed to get into the bath as fast as possible if we wanted to have a water birth.

I helped Anna-Marie out of bed and into the birthing bath. After her next contraction, Anna-Marie's parents arrived, just in time to see the crowning. Two contractions later, our baby girl was born. She was perfectly healthy and arrived in the midst of joyous emotion. We stayed at the birth house for another four hours and then went home with our little one.

When we got there, we saw that Aden was back from my father's and having his afternoon nap. After he woke, we immediately introduced him to his new little sister. We also gave him a gift and told him his sister had brought it with her especially for him. He was very impressed and very protective of her from the start. He sat with her in his arms for long periods of time and whenever someone else wanted to hold her or touch her, he told them, "No, that's *my* sister." We were so glad that he accepted her with such love and care. He was a real big brother. To this day, he is still very protective and brother and sister love one another very much. Ruana is absolutely infatuated with Aden and laughs at everything he does.

We used different donors for our two children for various reasons, but they look very much alike and we are raising them as brother and sister, even if they are only related through love. Anna-Marie and I were able to have them without too many issues. We are both registered as their parents on their birth certificates, which means we do not have to go through the long process of second-parent adoption.

It's now more than half a year after our daughter's birth. Our lives are so full with our two children. There are still some challenges and trials, as with everything else in life, but we wouldn't change our family for anything in the world. We love our children unconditionally and will do anything to make them happy, keep them safe and help them to reach their full potential.

# Lois D'Imperio and Holly Robinson

DANBURY, CONNECTICUT

I'm not sure how the discussion first started about kids. I liked kids, but wasn't so sure I was capable of raising them without incident. I'd been a good dog owner, but hadn't been able to keep a single goldfish or plant alive. I was quite skeptical of my ability to be a mom. But my partner, Lois, was great at it. She was sensible, practical, fun and organized—all of the things I thought it took to be a great mom.

Lois was a little gun-shy, though. She had pursued a court action for visitation with her twins (she had no legal rights or biological connection) and had felt really devastated about losing them. She did have very limited visitation, but no recognition as a mother. I think the hesitation at that point was more of her just needing a promise from me that we were going to work at our relationship and always put the best interest of the kids first. We were both on the same page with that, so soon she was ready to start looking for a donor.

We tried the "find a willing male friend" route first. We had two different friends we talked into being a part of the baby-making process. I went through the steps of creating necessary legal documents to make sure that the man couldn't be a "dad" and that this was solely a contractual relationship: sperm for money.

But the whole thing just didn't feel right. I didn't want the biological father to be someone the child knew. Both guys also felt torn about not having any relationship with the child at all. That's when I discussed the dilemma with our very awesome gay rights attorney and she strongly urged me to use an anonymous donor through a clinic for legal and medical reasons.

Picking the mom was the easy part: Lois is nine years older than me and didn't want to be having a baby when she was in her forties, so she went first. Next we had to find a donor. When we sat down at the computer, Lois prepared me for a long, drawn-out process. "This may take weeks," she warned.

When we first started exploring assisted reproduction, we talked to the OB/GYN and she immediately suggested that Lois take a cyto-megalovirus (CMV) test. This test showed that Lois was CMV negative. Therefore, due to scientific and medical mumbo jumbo that I don't under-stand, our donor had to be CMV negative as well.

So now we had some parameters based on Lois's family medical history and some physical attributes in my own lineage. The donor had to be CMV negative, without a history of Alzheimer's or diabetes and of some European descent. That was really it.

We found two guys in less than ten minutes. And that's where we started arguing.

I liked the philosopher/chef guy and Lois liked the oh-so-cute musi-cian guy. We had pages and pages of profiles for each of them. My straight girlfriends were blown away by how much we knew about the donors. They don't even know that much about their husbands! Lois and I spent the weekend discussing our two candidates and then, first thing Monday morning, Lois called to order the cute musician's sperm. It was sold out, so we went with the insightful thinker guy instead.

The actual insemination wasn't simple. Lois had a history of cervi-cal cancer and her treatments had affected her cervix to an extent. The first step was to dilate her cervix without anesthesia, which wasn't fun. Then we had to coordinate the sperm pick-up with the ovulation. Since our doctor's office didn't have a storage facility, we had the sperm sent to a fertility center in our state. It was fifty-five miles from our house and fifty miles from the doctor's office.

Once we had the timing down, Lois drove to pick up the sperm and then brought it in a cooler of dry ice to the OB/GYN, usually talking to the sperm and singing Melissa Etheridge to it the entire way. The IUI worked on the first try. While I was scared but excited, Lois was more reserved. She simply said one day, "I'm not feeling connected. I'm not feeling like this is the baby we're going to raise."

At thirteen weeks, Lois had a miscarriage. I was devastated, but Lois seemed really calm and was totally accepting of it. Unfortunately, not all was smooth sailing afterward. The doctor on call the weekend of the miscarriage advised us not to come in and suggested we just let nature take its course. It was a horrible weekend.

Four weeks later, Lois found herself in the emergency room with a doctor telling her "You have to go in for surgery right away. You're not bleeding out in my ER!" After that night, we both seemed to be really accepting of what had happened and were ready to move on.

After five more failed attempts using this sperm, we sat down with our OB/GYN for a consultation. She simply said, "Why not try a new donor? Some things just aren't meant to be."

So that night, we went back online and discovered that the cute musician was back on the market. Lois got pregnant on the first try and she stayed pregnant this time around. Due to her ripe old age of thirty-eight and the cervical cancer history, we had a ton of doctor check-ups along the way. Just when we thought things were going great (Lois was twenty-eight weeks along), she was told at a routine visit that she had to be put on immediate bed rest. She couldn't even drive home.

So we went into "strict bed rest" mode. We borrowed a cot bed from a friend and set up our living room for the patient. Lois didn't move except to go to the bathroom. I often went to work in the morning and left her two travel mugs of coffee, a laptop, a cooler of lunch and snacks and the TV remote. Sometimes, I didn't get home until late and found Lois hanging out in the dark, too afraid to get up to turn the light on.

"I didn't have to pee and didn't want to waste a trip getting out of bed," she said. It was not nearly as fun as one might think and I'm sure she wanted to jump down every person's throat who said, "Oh, lie down for eight weeks and watch TV; how hard can that be?" Lois is not someone who wastes time. It was a brutal experience for her.

At thirty-six weeks, the bed rest was finally lifted and Lois felt sure that the baby was just going to fall right out. But no matter what she tried, that kid didn't arrive until three weeks later—in tornado-like fashion. For all of our pre-delivery preparations and conversations with the doctor about medication and Lois's fear of pain, nothing really went as planned.

Lois's water started breaking at 3:00 P.M. on a Wednesday (she didn't tell me until 6:00 P.M., because she didn't want me to leave work early).

It *really* broke at 7:30 P.M. right in front of the burger joint she just *had to have* that evening. We got to the hospital around 9:00 P.M. and then Andrew was born at 12:07 A.M. There was no time for drugs, no time for anything, really. The one anesthesiologist on duty was busy with an appendectomy and despite Lois continuously calling out "NUUUURSE!" during labor, she never showed up to give Lois drugs.

The State of Connecticut had recently released a new birth certificate form prior to Andrew being born, so children of same-sex couples could have both of their parents listed on the form. It had something to the effect of "Parent 1" and "Parent 2" instead of "Mother" and "Father." The hospital didn't have those forms yet, so I called our gay rights lawyer who advised that I get one from the appropriate state agency. The nurses at the hospital weren't aware of the new form, but they were nice about it. We had a form faxed to them and became the first parents at the hospital to use the new certificate.

After we brought Andrew home and had a little time to settle in, the hospital social worker came to visit Lois and talk to her, since that was the protocol for a "single mom." Lois kept arguing with her, saying "I'm not a single mom! I'm married under state law and Holly is a parent under state law." But the woman kept insisting Lois was a single mom. It was annoying, but we just let her give her spiel after arguing didn't get us anywhere.

Wanting to have a second child meant that it was my turn to carry the baby. I was indifferent about being pregnant. I never thought I'd really do it. But I wanted a kid, so it was time to step up. Our OB/GYN was excited about our story. "How great that each of you gets to experience this!" she said. "Do you know how many of my patients would love to have their *husbands* go through a pregnancy, too?"

I got pregnant on the first try—our donor had super sperm. Like the first time, we found out the baby's gender when we could. I thought we were having a girl all along until the morning of the ultrasound. I woke up, turned to Lois and said, "It's totally a boy." And it was.

My pregnancy was fairly uneventful. I had morning sickness for almost four months—just constantly nauseous—and heartburn all the time. I worked a half day one Friday in November and left early for a doctor appointment—it was six days before my due date. My blood pressure was high, so I did a few more blood tests over the weekend. On Monday morning, we were instructed to report to the hospital to be induced.

As we settled into the delivery room, we told the nurse about Lois giving birth in the same room. The nurse came back a few minutes later with a big grin on her face and said, "You're not going to believe me, but the anesthesiologist on duty tonight is the same one Lois had and she's scheduled for an appendectomy again."

She wasn't kidding. The anesthesiologist missed the opportunity to give me drugs, too.

I think it's pretty amazing that we have two boys who have biological traits from both of us, but I don't think it makes any difference to them or us who gave birth to whom. Our firstborn was a very tough, stubborn, colicky baby. He definitely seemed to be spirited very early on in his life—and still is. So when we decided to have a second child, we were a little more confident that we could handle it.

We are doing everything we can to raise these boys with compassion, resiliency and a good moral compass. I sometimes feel like my seven-year-old is a little restless, but just yesterday his speech teacher stopped me in the hallway of his school to tell me what a sweet, kind boy he is. I was blown away and later told my son how proud I was.

Right now we live in a very diverse community. We are surrounded by families of all kinds of races, religions and beliefs. Both of our boys have been accepted in every school and sport they've joined. We've become involved in their activities, including coaching T-ball and soccer in the past few years.

Our families are incredible. Our friends are wonderful. Our neighbors are fantastic. I can honestly say that Lois and I have been met with more responses of "That's cool!" or "Okay, great!" when we've explained that we're both the moms.

Today we are almost at our fourteen-year anniversary. We have a great relationship with each other (although Lois cringes at the words "wife" or "marriage" from time to time). We worry about money and work opposite schedules so one of us is usually home with the boys. It's been hard since our time together as a family is fairly infrequent—my wife works nights and weekends and I work fifty hours, Monday through Friday—but we're making it work.

They are both amazing boys and we are very lucky to be where we are. Our state and the community in which we live have been truly remarkable. We have stories on top of stories about our lives with these boys. They are so different in personality, but both full of energy and spirit. As with any kids, we have moments of frustration and insanity, followed by moments of incredible gratitude.

# Jenn and Michele Margiotta-Watz

SHOREHAM, NEW YORK

My name is Jenn and I have always known I wanted to be a mom. I am one of thirty-one grandchildren on my mother's side alone—a large family that has generations which overlap in age. I was babysitting cousins when I was ten years old and loved being around babies.

My wife's road to parenthood started when she lost her partner of eighteen years to cancer and realized she was all alone. Michele had no one else to recount the good times with, to remember the vacations and laughs shared. It was the first time she wished for a child—someone who could tell her story after she was gone.

Michele and I moved in together in 2001 and enjoyed going to musical concerts, theater, travelling and living in our legally-unrecognized "marital" bliss. As sappy as it sounds, we had so much love in our hearts for each other that we wanted to share that love with a child. While we certainly weren't considered "in the closet" at the time, we did want to start our own family and have a child with whom we could share our lives.

Knowing we wanted to have a family and that I definitely wanted to carry our child, we began to look at sperm banks. Neither of us was comfortable with knowing the donor personally or having him remain a part of our child's life, so we decided to use an anonymous donor. We felt that with all the love we had to offer our child between the two of us, the lack of a biological father wouldn't be missed. And happily, today we can say that while the absence has been acknowledged, it has not been more than a passing thought.

So with the Internet at our disposal, we started looking for the perfect donor. It was amazing to see all of the details that were readily available online. Obviously there were the physical characteristics like eye color, height and hair color, but also their SAT scores, short answers on their favorite childhood holidays, college majors and even their GPAs. Another discriminating factor that's made available to potential buyers is the donor's educational status. When we were purchasing our vials, the sperm collected from those with graduate degrees was more expensive than others.

When we decided we had found the donor we wanted to use and were ready to start actively trying to conceive, it was 2004. We began living our lives in two-week cycles. The first two weeks were waiting to ovulate and then the next two were waiting to see if I got my period or a positive test. It was an exercise in patience—something you need in spades as a parent.

In the two weeks leading up to ovulation, I took my basal body temperature daily (there was supposed to be a slight increase which signaled ovulation), although I didn't find this methodology very helpful. It's also suggested to check for a thinning of cervical mucus as your body prepares to ovulate. But my failsafe for determining ovulation was the standard ovulation kits. They work similarly to any pregnancy test you can find at the drugstore. These kits measure a hormone that spikes just before ovulation, but they aren't cheap. Most kits come with only five or seven pee sticks, so once I got pretty good at judging my cycle, I managed to stretch one box across two cycles (provided the expiration date cooperated).

At the time we were trying to conceive, New York State regulations were significantly more relaxed, so we could practice self-insemination at home. As long as the sperm was signed for and delivered to a licensed physician's office, all was good. I had a wonderful relationship with my general practitioner and her office received the large liquid nitrogen tank containing our vials of sperm and allowed me to bring it home. I remember driving down the road with the large tank buckled into my passenger seat. The inseminations themselves were as easy as every "lesbian with a turkey baster" joke implies.

After we had completed the insemination, we were responsible for shipping the tank back to the cryobank. The most accessible drop-off location for us on the commute to work together had a gal working there who we assumed was "on our team." She had a very butch haircut, never wore make-up and was always wearing cargo shorts. We weren't ones to make assumptions about a person's sexual preference, but we always felt this woman "got it" whenever we dropped off the tank. One day she casually mentioned that she had shipped a tank like that from a local horse farm—they ordered sperm for their mare. Clearly she "got it." We smiled and parted ways.

I used pregnancy tests as early as detection was advised on the box and continued until my menstruation started. After trying for several months, we were elated to find out I was pregnant. It had worked! A doctor's trip and blood test confirmed that one of those frozen swimmers had made its way to my egg.

It was Valentine's Day weekend 2005, and we had our first sonogram scheduled—but there was no heartbeat. I was crushed. Even now I can hear the doctor's words echoing in the room and feeling like all the air had been sucked out. I was depressed and convinced it was something I had done wrong that resulted in our loss. In reality, that wasn't the case, but it still took a lot of time and reading to heal—miscarriage rates are significantly underrepresented, in my opinion. My wife was very supportive during this time—it was her loss too, after all—but it deeply affected me on a personal level to know that I had a life within me that was snuffed out so quickly after being so jubilantly received.

We waited a few months after that, as I needed to heal both physically and emotionally before trying to conceive again. We knew that our desire to be parents was stronger than our fear. Today we know that being a parent is all about facing your fears.

It was about that time when the State of New York changed its regulations on where frozen sperm could be delivered, essentially restricting it to reproductive specialists who performed inseminations in an office exam room. So I no longer would have the chance to say my wife "got me pregnant." Gone were the comforts of home—my pillows, comforter, a glass of wine to share. I now wore a paper gown during conception on a table covered in tissue paper.

Working for a large hospital system, I had access to some of the best doctors in the country, some just down the road from my laboratory. We met with my new reproductive doctor and his team with great hope—these people make their living by making babies. Getting pregnant was a carefully-timed dance. I used ovulation sticks exclusively to chart my progress and when I was within twenty-four hours of ovulation, I called the office and made an appointment for the next day. The appointments were time-dependent on whether the test was positive in the morning or afternoon.

This significantly more scientific version of having a baby included multiple sonograms and measuring the egg itself. But the essential difference was that we were no longer using intracervical insemination (ICI) as we did at home; we were now working with washed sperm and the doctor used a catheter to perform intrauterine insemination (IUI) to get closer to the fallopian tubes.

I was able to conceive again that summer, but it was short-lived and I miscarried within a week of getting a positive test. After this happened a third time, I learned it was referred to as a chemical pregnancy—when the β-subunit of human chorionic gonadotropin (beta-hCG) levels rise, but there are no anatomical signs of pregnancy (an embryonic sac). The rate of this type of miscarriage is hard to judge, because unless you are taking lots of pregnancy tests and being followed by a specialist, most women believe they are just late and then get their period without ever knowing their hormone levels had gone up.

Unfortunately for us, we knew immediately when I was pregnant and this steep emotional rollercoaster of elation followed by devastation was maddening. My doctor suggested doing some genetic testing to make sure there were no other factors contributing to my multiple miscarriages. The tests came back negative and I was cleared to start trying to conceive again.

Some of the strangest coffee breaks happened in those months of trying to conceive. I often left work to "go get coffee," but instead went to the clinic and got inseminated before stepping back into work happy and hopeful. It was shortly after the genetic testing that I became pregnant again. And I'm happy to say this was the one that finally stuck!

We live and work on Long Island, infamous for its traffic. By the fourth month of my pregnancy, I knew every bathroom spanning thirty-plus exits on the Long Island Expressway. Overall, I had a rather uneventful pregnancy. I did have gestational diabetes, but testing my blood sugar by sticking myself four times a day was a small price to pay for the miracle I was carrying.

Before we knew it, October 2006 rolled around and I was waddling everywhere. I drove myself to the doctor's office, not knowing that my water had broken and that I was leaking amniotic fluid. My labor was stalled and our son was so comfortable inside me that we needed a stimulant to help my labor progress. I chose to receive an epidural to help me with the pain and within hours we were the proud parents of a baby boy. Michele and I knew that as a parent you love your child, but we had no idea the voracity that one loves with—Shane was and is our heart.

Adjusting to parenthood came with its own set of challenges. The delirium from lack of sleep is something that cannot be explained, only experienced. Some mothers idealize their delivery plan and when life deviates from that plan, they are torn apart. I knew our son's birth story meant little to me in the way of specifics, only that he and I were healthy in the end.

My personal nemesis was breastfeeding. I desperately wanted to nurse our son, but Mother Nature did not share in my vision. I worked with lactation consultants and used a supplemental nursing system but, at the end of the day, I was limited by what my body was capable of producing. Even as I write this, over seven years after these events occurred, I am still disappointed in my body for betraying my deepest desires.

But in the grand scheme of things, this "hiccup" in my parenting abilities was inconsequential. Our son was a happy and healthy baby and he lulled us into a false sense of security in our parenting skills…so we decided to have another baby! Our decision to expand our family further actually came at a very sad time—while watching siblings grieve over the loss of their mother (a close friend of the family). We knew that we didn't want our son to be alone when we passed.

We had already picked out our donor and it made sense for Shane to have a full sibling, as I was happy to carry again. Conceiving our second child was a much different experience, because I was now toting a toddler with me to my reproductive office. Nothing says "family" like having a kid strapped into a stroller next to you as your feet are raised in stirrups.

Luckily for us, this second attempt worked quickly and I became pregnant within four cycles. Managing my hormones and our toddler's tantrums was a balancing act my wife somehow accomplished without going completely insane. I again had gestational diabetes, but with chasing a toddler around I had gotten used to doing everything on the fly. When it came to labor, we requested that I be induced during my last week of pregnancy as a matter of convenience and babysitting availability. Michele was very concerned about taking care of me while simultaneously tending to our son, a feeling of pressure that was alleviated by my mother's arrival. In May 2009, again with the aid of a labor stimulant, I delivered a healthy baby boy, Ian.

Parenting our first, then parenting our second and the dynamic between the two has been a whole different ballgame. Our sons make us smile every day. They are so different in their personalities and each is funny, intelligent and sweet. We keep a composition notebook of all the cute, entertaining and exasperating moments they have blessed us with over the last seven years.

I leave you with a story from the backseat of a minivan. A friend of mine was taking our older son to music class while I stayed home with our infant and an injured foot. As Shane and my friend's son chatted in the backseat, the statement was made: "You don't have a dad." From the front seat, my friend listened with baited breath, ready to intervene and steer the conversation if needed. But our son replied in his happy, sweet way: "No, I have two moms. We are a family."

# PART 5
# CO-PARENTING

When same-sex couples decide to have children, it is common for them to look into adoption, surrogacy, foster care or assisted reproduction. Not many people think about or even know about co-parenting. Co-parenting is when two or more people in a platonic relationship raise children together. It's most commonly seen when heterosexual couples separate but still have joint custody of their children. However, there are other instances where individuals decide to co-parent without ever being romantically involved. Think of it as a shared custody scenario without the ugly divorce.

Whenever additional people are involved in raising the child, there are many opportunities to create a more balanced life. While one parent or couple is taking care of the child, the other person or couple can catch up on things like sleep, chores, work-related activities or hobbies. This allows you to be more focused on your child when he or she is present. Because there is shared custody, you can also have free time while your child is staying with his or her other parents. This makes it easier to schedule date nights and have more alone time with your partner.

If you choose to co-parent, you're not going through the journey alone and you can use the support of your co-parenting partners when difficult situations arise.

When two sets of parents are raising a child, if each of them is working there will be four incomes to help with the expenses of child care. This can alleviate a lot of financial stress if it is clear upfront how each person is going to contribute.

For some people, having a biological connection with their child is important. In a co-parenting situation, it is possible for both biological parents to take active roles in raising the child. Everyone involved also has the opportunity to witness and be a part of the pregnancy journey. It is possible for them to be present for sonograms, for the baby's first heart-beat and maybe even to feel the baby kick. Finally, if everyone is comfort-able with it and the doctors allow it, each of you can be present during the birth.

A well-thought-out co-parenting scenario can be great for everyone involved, including the children; however, that doesn't mean there aren't risks associated with it. If the moms have one set of rules at their house and the dads have another set of rules at theirs, things can get compli-cated very quickly. Jealousy can even creep in if people are not secure in the parenting relationship structure they've created. That can result in an uncomfortable situation for everyone involved. Making sure everyone is on the same page in the beginning will make things easier later on down the road.

It may not seem like an issue in the beginning, but if the other couple (or person) you co-parent with lives a fair distance away, this could even-tually turn into a hassle or major inconvenience. Some people choose to live very close to each other or even in the same home to avoid this. Also, it may not always be possible for everyone to be together during the holidays. Consider how this will impact you and your children. Keep in mind that extended family members may be disappointed with not being together during these times, too. What if one of you has to move to another city, state or country for work or other reasons? This could complicate your joint custody plans as well.

Finally, it is important to note that there can be legal complications, too. Only a few states acknowledge that a child can have more than two legally-recognized parents. You may be able to do a third-parent adoption in some states, but it's best to consult with a lawyer to fully understand your rights.

The stories in this section detail the benefits and challenges that come with co-parenting. They also highlight the importance of having proper legal protections in place and making sure everyone is on the same page before starting this journey.

# Paul and Dustin

SAN JOSE, CALIFORNIA

"You should write a book!"

It was the Spring of 2009 and we'd heard that statement countless times ever since our first daughter was born almost three years prior. My husband and I had just taken part in a prospective parent discussion group at a nearby LGBT Center. There were eight attendees, all gay men and women in various stages of planning their own families. Dustin and I were there to offer insight into a form of parenting that few people knew much about: intentional co-parenting. We have two daughters and are raising them with their two mothers. The four of us are collectively known as our daughters' Parental Entourage.

Until recent years, the phrase "co-parenting" applied almost exclusively to divorced parents who shared equal custody of their kids. Look it up online and that's mostly what you'll find. But those are all unintentional co-parenting situations. The parents never planned to raise their kids as a separated couple. And in most of those cases, the children's lives are disrupted due to the parents' split. Even in the cases where the divorce is amicable, the lives of the children are still altered midstream. They lived in one home with two parents and then suddenly they're in two homes with one parent and maybe an eventual stepparent or two.

That's not the case with intentional co-parenting, where shared custody is the norm beginning at birth. One of the commonalities of all LGBT parents is the need to think outside the box when planning for a family. There are all the usual routes: adoption, surrogate mothers, sperm donor dads, in vitro fertilization. And they can be done whether single or coupled. But for many prospective parents, even all those options may not be ideal. Cost is always one of the biggest prohibitive factors. And not just for the conception, adoption and all the legalities that are involved, but for the subsequent care of the child as well. There is also the strain of the latter, since raising children—or more accurately, future adults—is no minor task. But having children doesn't have to be just for those who can afford it and caring for them doesn't have to be a Herculean effort. Co-parenting can be a successful way to share that immense responsibility.

However, children aren't objects to be co-owned like a time-share, so isn't it wrong to bring them into such a family structure? Not if done right. And all indications are that we baby daddies and baby mamas are doing it right. Here's a bit of our story, how we formed our family and how the four of us work together to ensure our girls thrive.

Dustin and I began dating in 1997. Dustin was thirty-three, I was thirty and we were living in a small apartment in New York's East Village. Parenting was never an expectation that we or our families had for us. Dustin has always loved kids and they have always been drawn to him; I say he's like a human cartoon character because of the crazy facial expressions he can make. But having our own children? Oh, heck no; not us! We were socially active guppies (gay urban professionals) enjoying our youth and freedom.

I was okay with never having children and thought Dustin felt the same. But it turned out that his love of kids ran deep enough that by our late thirties, after having settled down in San Jose, his biological alarm clock started going off. We began having discussions that weren't thrilling me. I knew myself: I didn't have the level of selflessness needed to be an effective, successful, full-time parent. My own upbringing made me even more cynical. My parents had my oldest brother by accident after dating for only a short time. They weren't ready for one kid, yet within six years they had four. The next twenty-plus years were dysfunctional enough to have left a bad impression on me. So if I couldn't commit myself to being the most attentive possible parent, if I didn't feel that strong parental drive that many others feel, then I wasn't going to bring an innocent life into the world just to save my relationship.

By early 2004, the decision was final—we weren't having kids. I was relieved. Dustin seemed disappointed, but eventually got over it. Or so it seemed on the surface. One evening, I came home from work and found that Dustin had been crying, which he'd been doing all day, he said. Initially, I thought it had to do with some minor tension we'd had the night before. Instead, he said he was mourning the thought of never having kids. The finality of our decision had confirmed that his desire was very real and deeply rooted. He looked at his future and saw a void that was never going to be filled.

Dustin has always been family-oriented. Our home is full of mementos from his parents, grandparents and great-grandparents. On an almost daily basis, he uses folksy phrases he learned from his grandparents as a child; he uses them so frequently they've worked their way into my own daily lexicon.

Images came to my mind of an eighty-year-old Dustin without kids or grandkids of his own, his parents long gone and his sister and her family living elsewhere in the country. If I was dead and no longer in the picture, the thought of him alone broke my heart. I considered relenting, but still couldn't do it. We're talking about an innocent life being brought into the world without choice or adopted into our home just to assuage the guilt of one man and to prevent the potential loneliness of another.

The "no kids" decision remained in place.

Dustin mourned while I felt guilty and mulled over the little twinge of dread that our relationship might suffer as a result. But in the dictionary, there is a photo of Dustin next to the word "tenacity" and in truth, he had never really considered the "no kids" decision as final. By mid-2004, as we were right on the verge of purchasing our first home, Dustin stumbled across an online posting by a woman looking for prospective dads for co-parenting. It's something we'd heard of previously, but didn't give it much consideration—we couldn't think of any women in our life who wanted children, let alone wanted to raise them with us.

It had certainly seemed like the ideal compromise for us. Not having to take care of the kid 24/7? Days off during the week to rest and recover? Sharing the financial burdens? And best of all, multiple parents to compensate for my inevitable shortcomings as a father? The concept was too good to be true! Being able to "have a life" while also having kids was something I could see myself agreeing to, but it was pure fantasy at that point.

Dustin had been poking around online one weekend afternoon and brought up how he just "happened" to stumble across a posting from a lesbian looking to meet single or coupled gay men for the purpose of co-parenting. He asked if I was open enough to at least meet with her and find out more. With images of a retired and lonely Dustin still floating through my head and a very strong curiosity about co-parenting, I agreed to keep an open mind and check it out. After all, it wasn't like it was going to lead to anything, right?

We composed an introduction e-mail together right then and sent it off. The woman responded within twenty-four hours and within a week, we were sitting in her living room. I was amazed at how nervous Dustin was. He's typically a gregarious guy, yet as we sat on the couch, he struggled to speak. And his body language—wow! If he crossed his legs and wrapped his arms around himself any tighter, he might have turned blue! I swear his teeth were chattering. Overall, the conversation went well. She shared some details of her experiences searching for a co-parent, including how there were a couple of strong prospects who hadn't worked out. She had tried other venues without success and then she thought of putting something online. The posting that Dustin found was her first attempt and it had received only a few nibbles.

Thanks to this woman, we learned you don't need to limit yourself to people you know when looking for a co-parent. Co-parents can be found the old-fashioned way: through want ads and subsequent dating. Yes, dating. Only instead of looking for the love of your life, you're looking for someone who shares your vision of having and raising children. As with romantic relationships, compatible personalities and the ability to communicate are essential. The way to find out if you have that compatibility is through dating, which usually begins with a brief face-to-face meeting over a cup of coffee or a drink, like we were having now.

Things didn't work out with her in the end, but as a result of that meeting, we learned about an informal group called Prospective Queer Parents (PQP). Through a bare-bones website, people could volunteer to host one of the monthly potlucks where prospective parents could mix and mingle. We attended our first one in February 2004 and had no clue what to expect. The potluck began with everyone grabbing a bite to eat, then sitting in a circle, group-counseling-session style.

We went around the room and introduced ourselves and explained our vision of the ideal family. It seemed the most common thing being looked for among the women was a known donor, but not one who wanted to be a legal father. Their children could know their father and see him on some limited, agreed-upon conditions, but he would have no custodial rights or decision-making authority. As luck had it, that was in line with what most of the men seemed to be looking for. They didn't necessarily want to be a legal or full-time parent, but they did want to have steady contact with their children and to fill the role of primary male role model. Since we wanted full shared legal custody, that made slim pickings for us among the prospective moms, but at least there was less competition from the prospective dads.

After everyone was introduced, the host said a couple of things to kick-start the conversation. The discussions covered the entire spectrum of planning for procreation and child-rearing: fertility testing and troubles with conceiving, costs of insemination, sperm donors, avenues of adoption and referrals to various lawyers, doctors, adoption agencies, clinics and sperm banks. Discipline, nutrition, birth techniques, custody laws, grandparents, nursery decorating—all that and more was discussed in due time.

With traditional married couples, even those of the same sex, half of these answers are known or at least assumed. If you marry someone, it's almost a built-in assumption that you might want to have kids with them or that their approach to child-rearing is in line with your own. For those looking at parenting options outside of the two-parent, one-household model, there can be no assumptions. Every angle needs to be explored and hammered out.

It was a tremendously informative support group we were relieved to have found. But there was this odd undercurrent running through the meetings. While we were all supportive and sympathetic, many of us were technically competing with each other. The women wanted fathers and the men wanted mothers. So this parenting support group was also part meat market, the local pick-up bar with a twelve-step component. After the introductions were made and the conversation got underway, we started sizing each other up. Outwardly, we might be discussing prenatal healthcare, but inwardly we were thinking, "Would she be a good mother? Does he look like a reliable father?"

In spite of our first two dating scenarios not going anywhere, our parenting quest was proving at least interesting and educational, so we kept going. Our next PQP meeting was on April 18, 2004. The majority of attendees were new faces from the prior meeting: "fresh meat." We did the rounds of introductions and one of the last to speak was Daisy. She explained how she was in the early stages of research on becoming a parent. She was open to various options, but as she was single, she was leaning most strongly toward co-parenting. Bingo! As with our previous PQP meeting, there appeared to be opportunity for success.

After the formal conversation had wrapped up, we began the casual mixing and mingling. A handful of us were standing in a circle, chatting. Daisy and I were maybe two or three people apart and stealing glances at each other. Over time, we inched our way closer to each other and finally had the chance for one-on-one introductions and small talk. And yes, the description above sounds very much like—and felt very much like—when you are attracted to someone at a party and work your way over to them in the hopes the attraction is mutual. In this case, it was. By the time we left, Dustin and Daisy had exchanged e-mail information and we left with the standard, non-committal line, "We should get together sometime."

At 2:50 P.M. the next day, Daisy e-mailed us asking if we wanted to meet and talk over coffee. Wait, isn't it a sign of desperation to write to someone you're interested in the very next day? The rule is to wait at least forty-eight hours so you don't come across as too interested. But maybe that's just for romantic dating and not prospective-parent dating, so we responded right away. After some scheduling conflicts, we finally had our first date and this time it was followed up by a second and then a third.

We had already been scheduled to host the next PQP potluck, which coincidentally fell on Father's Day. The turnout was about the usual dozen or so people, but this time there were no prospective moms who stood out to us. We interpreted that as fate. Daisy couldn't make it to the potluck, so there were no distractions from the continuation of our courtship. After a few more dates, Dustin suggested the idea of a weekly "family night," where we could get to know Daisy without the constant need to find space on the calendar.

Family nights (or more accurately, family planning nights) were sometimes casual and included having dinner, going bowling, seeing a movie or getting to know each other's friends. Other nights we intentionally focused on discussions of what we were looking for in a co-parent, what our expectations were regarding shared custody, how we planned to approach child-rearing, options for conceiving, the legal steps necessary to cover everyone involved and more.

We were enjoying our family nights together and eventually felt confident enough to ask Daisy if she was satisfied and wanted to make babies with us. Turns out she had already decided it was a done deal. For her, our connection just felt right. So there it was—we were having a baby.

By that point, we already knew Daisy had some personal goals she wanted to reach before having her first child. So we needed to wait a while longer before taking the next concrete steps. That was just as well, since the following months turned out to be a pretty eventful time for all of us, with personal challenges and loss.

On October 30, 2004, Dustin started feeling achy all over. His neck and shoulders were cramped, which in turn gave him headaches. This had happened before, with stress being the cause. The following day it became worse and the pain started spreading to other parts of his body. This new pain was nothing he had experienced before, so we headed to the hospital. The doctors ran some tests on him but couldn't figure out what was wrong and sent him home for the night. The next day, Dustin was admitted to the hospital and underwent further testing. The results came back that Wednesday, so I left work early to hear the news and arrived while Dustin was sleeping.

He eventually woke up, but was in a morphine stupor. We made some hasty greetings and at his request, I helped him sit up on the edge of the bed. He asked if I'd heard about the test results. I said I knew they were in, but I didn't know what they were. He grimaced a bit and told me he was HIV positive. A wave of relief passed over me. Odd reaction, right? Not really. First, there was the relief that we finally had an answer, something definite that could be dealt with. The uneasiness of our not knowing was finally lifted. Also, Dustin could benefit from all the advances made in treating HIV. It wasn't a death sentence anymore, just a really crappy chronic illness that he had to keep in check with lifelong daily medications. But at least that life could be long. I assured him that we'd deal with it together. His energy quickly faded and he went back to sleep while I resumed watching him from the bedside chair.

Then it hit me: Dustin was just three short weeks from his fortieth birthday. He was already not thrilled about that, since he's more like a twenty-year-old at heart. Now he would have to reach that dreaded milestone as someone living with HIV. It was not going to be a very happy birthday.

That realization saddened me and I got choked up. And then an even bigger realization hit—Dustin couldn't father a child of his own now. Hitting forty and becoming HIV positive was going to be a real blow to this man who had such eternal optimism. Then heap on top of that the loss of this dream when we were so close and I couldn't imagine Dustin's reaction once he was coherent enough for it to sink in. The thought was heart-wrenching and by that point I had already become excited by the prospect of a little Dustin running around, an excitement that was now reinforced with a layer of urgency due to the scary nature of these past few days. The scary thought of his passing away was slightly less painful if a piece of him remained. But now that prospect was gone.

Dustin woke briefly and gave me a quizzical look. I forced a smile through my now tear-streaked face. I was counting on the low light and his drug-induced stupor to hide the fact that I was crying. He drifted away quickly and I went into the bathroom, where I ended up kneeling on the floor, sobbing uncontrollably like some over-the-top soap opera actor.

The next day Dustin was far more coherent and we were able to discuss his diagnosis and treatment in detail with his doctors. As the days passed, his condition improved. The pain went down and he regained his strength, so we were able to start discussing what all of this meant to us and our future. How would this news affect Daisy's decision to have kids with us? It wasn't just Dustin's inability to father a child that could now hamper our plans; it was also the possibility that the woman we'd spent so much time building a relationship with might not want to raise kids with someone who was HIV positive. And if she didn't, would we be able to meet someone else willing to create a family with us?

Early on in our talks with Daisy, we had all decided to have two children together. Over time, the idea was proposed for Dustin to father the first child and then I the second. So now, under these new circumstances, it didn't take much to determine that I would just father both kids. It wasn't ideal for me, since much of my excitement about having kids had revolved around the thought of a little Dustin.

When we finally broke the news to Daisy, we included the suggestion of having me father both kids and said we understood if she wasn't comfortable with going forward. Fortunately, Daisy isn't prudish or delicate. She had a few concerns, naturally, but her overall reaction was just a shrug and the attitude of adapting to the situation. What a relief! We could now check that off the list of concerns as we moved forward with addressing Dustin's new health status.

Next we started to formalize all of our discussions into a written parenting agreement. During this period of calm, cool collectedness, we pondered every aspect of parenting and came to agreements on how to handle them: shared custody, holidays, names, religion, circumcision, health care and insurance, taxes, finances and schooling. We tried to approach all topics from every possible angle.

When the time came to announce that we were going to have kids, Dustin's parents and my mom were elated (My dad had passed away a couple of years earlier). But they also had some questions for us as well: Were we going to adopt or ask a surrogate to carry the baby? If the latter, then which of us was going to father the child? Those were fair questions and ones that even heterosexual couples are asked if they can't conceive biologically. But when Dustin and I said that we planned to co-parent with a woman we had met less than a year ago, the inquiries about adoption and surrogates were nothing compared to the barrage of questions we were slammed with after that. Our friends were just as slack-jawed as our families.

I can't recall a single person we knew who had heard of co-parenting prior to our announcement. Considering all of the planning we had written into our parenting agreement, it was annoying when people asked about a list of worst-case scenarios, as if we hadn't put the least bit of thought into this:

"What if you divorce?"

"What if one of you gets a job across the country?"

"What if one of you dies?"

Yeesh! Can't you people just be happy for us and say "Congratulations"? Well, apparently not, but that was actually a good thing.

Yes, our friends and family understood that when people have kids, it's usually a happy occasion. But they were also concerned for us, since we were venturing into new territory with our approach. The reason why married couples aren't slammed with all of the same questions is that the worst-case scenarios have already been addressed extensively. You don't have to ask a married couple about what happens if they divorce, because we're already aware of how divorces are handled, whether amicable or not. And we don't ask a married couple if they're sure they want kids, because it's already assumed that marriage leads to babies (although this assumption should be challenged, since not every married couple truly wants kids or is prepared to have them).

But what about this new concept of intentional co-parenting, where the parents are not legally bound to each other, but just to their children? If one half of a married couple needs to move for a job, it's a given that the spouse and child will move as well. And if that doesn't happen, there are laws and precedents to address that. But unmarried parents don't have any such obligation to each other.

"Where will the children live?"

"Where will they go to school?"

"Which parent will pay for this or that?"

"Who will make the decisions about this or that?"

And the questions kept coming.

It didn't take long to get past the initial annoyance of endless questions and instead come to appreciate them. While we had considered most of the same concerns that our friends and family expressed, there were still nuggets of wisdom or uncovered areas that needed to be addressed and their feedback helped us hone in on them. So in the end, we are better parents because of it.

Dustin and I are now staunch advocates for any and all intrusive questioning of prospective parents. Raising a child is no insignificant endeavor. It is the responsibility of everyone in a prospective parent's life to grill him or her on his or her readiness to create a future adult human being. Miss Manners be damned if that's not proper etiquette.

Things went smoothly in 2005 as we continued to fine-tune our plans. Daisy bought her first home, the final goal she had set for herself prior to conceiving. Now there was nothing left to do but start making babies. All of the legal aspects were still being worked out, but those were just technicalities. To ensure that everyone was covered as best as possible, we met with a very well-known family lawyer in the area who specializes in alternative families. We also set up a joint savings account between the three of us and began depositing 5 percent (and then later 10 percent) of our gross salaries. We planned to use the joint account for all big-ticket childcare costs over the years—things like medical care, tuition and family travel. The respective parent was responsible for anything beyond the necessities, such as gifts and leisure-time activities.

We had also met with counselors both as a family and separately to address underlying issues. In hindsight, I suppose I should have spoken up about my still-lingering doubts regarding this baby-making business. That lack of courage eventually came back to bite me later on.

One twist that did take place that year came about when Daisy started dating someone. Prior to this, she had proposed a clause in our written parenting agreement that prevented any hypothetical partner from having parental authority for at least the first two years. After the two years, all three of us had to agree on extending equal authority, if Daisy's partner herself was even interested. This suggestion was a display of the pragmatism Dustin and I found reassuring in Daisy. We all know how the initial throes of love can cloud judgment and she willingly offered to protect against that. This clause also covers Dustin and I should there ever be a worst-case scenario between us (although that's really hard to imagine).

But everything in the written parenting agreement had been considered within a post-birth context. We hadn't considered the possibility of a hypothetical partner being around prior to insemination, let alone the birth. We decided to keep the clause in effect and hope for the best. We could discuss the matter in more detail when the baby was two years old. If Daisy's partner was around from day one, our child was naturally going to view her as another parent. What if the relationship didn't work out? Fortunately, that is a scenario we haven't had to deal with, as the moms are still together over eight years later.

As for the actual process of insemination, we had already determined that no medical intervention was required. All medical tests showed that both Daisy and I were healthy. Through research we had learned that, minus any health problems, there was a very high success rate for do-it-yourself insemination. It was also the most cost-effective way to go. Daisy had been tracking her cycle closely, so we knew the optimal dates of ovulation. Then she gave me a heads-up so I could "save up" on my end for the days beforehand. I'll skip the specifics of the actual process (which were pretty tame, so you can keep the imagination in check), but will admit there was a high degree of performance anxiety. No matter how romantic Dustin and I tried to make our half of the process, it was hard not to feel like a stud being used for breeding. It was all so mechanical. Where was the wine, the flowers, the Barry White?

The first couple of attempts were a bust and then there were some scheduling conflicts on the date of the third. Daisy called us early in the day and offered to reschedule due to these conflicts, but admitted she felt an indescribable sense that this time could be it. The mix of excitement and trepidation was clearly coming through in her voice. So we stuck with the plan and got together that night. There was definitely a vibe in the air. We all felt it. A few days later, Daisy said she felt as if her insides were being "renovated." In February 2006, the pregnancy strips told us we were with child.

*Wow. I guess we are really doing this.*

Immediately after confirming the pregnancy, Daisy signed us up for parenting and birthing classes offered through her insurance carrier. The classes covered everything from how the fetus develops, to breathing exercises during labor, to how to change diapers. No joke, these classes should be required for anyone planning to have children. If people have to study and practice to drive a car, then it should also be mandatory for raising future adults.

Daisy and Dustin both began doing heavy research into all aspects of parenting with various parenting books that were snatched up or given to us by friends and family. We attended the two sonogram appointments and saw the progression of our pending baby's development from the size of a kidney bean to the size of a potato. We were becoming the proud parents of a food item!

It had long been decided that we didn't want to learn the baby's sex before the birth. That certainly made it difficult for others to purchase advance gifts and we had to awkwardly refer to our child as "it" through-out the pregnancy. Added to the suspense was not knowing our baby's name. One of our earliest decisions was to have Daisy pick the first and middle names, selecting from her parents' and grandparents' names, whether we had a boy or a girl.

The last name was up to Dustin and me and we kicked around a couple of options. The first idea was simply hyphenating our last names. We also considered combining our last names and then possibly even changing our own to have the same last name as our kids. Friends had done this before and we saw that it worked for them. Dustin and I tried various combinations of the letters in our last names and came up with Delpar, Pardel, Delparney, Parlane and Delparish. Nothing was clicking. Then we combined the first three letters of my last name with the last three letters of Dustin's last name and struck gold—Delish! Imagine us introducing ourselves at parties, "Hi! We're the Delishes!"

In spite of the enthusiasm expressed by certain friends for "Delish," we ultimately went back to option number one: hyphenating our names for the kids and keeping our own last names.

Meanwhile, the baby research and preparation continued. We all went shopping to look at baby gear such as strollers, changing tables and car seats. More classes were taken and more legal legwork was done. Things were moving along as the excitement and anticipation built up. But for one of us, so did the apprehension and dread.

My nagging doubts about this whole endeavor hadn't completely subsided. The more that Daisy's belly expanded, the more real this whole thing became. There was now a very real possibility of all my worst fears coming true: I wasn't going to be a competent father for this person being brought into the world and the cycle that began with my father's parents and probably even prior was now going to continue with me—parents having kids they weren't capable of properly raising. Yes, he or she might have three other devoted parents, but it still didn't change the fact that one of them—and one of the biological ones, no less—probably wasn't up to it.

Since I have a penchant for over-thinking things, I figured that coming clean to Dustin would be the best way for me to purge those remaining doubts. It's usually all that's needed to do the trick. So about three months ahead of the baby's due date, I brought it up to him. Oh boy. Never had one of our heart-to-hearts devolved so quickly or become so heated. Within the first few sentences, Dustin asked if I was afraid I might resent him for our having kids. In a calm, non-accusatory way, I replied, "Yes, that's what I'm afraid of." In seconds, he was almost out the door while saying I could just leave now and that the rest of them would continue on without me. Yeesh!

Luckily, he didn't leave and we continued talking, but he was being very dismissive. He thought I should just get over it, because the baby was already coming. As we continued to talk, I found resentment building up. It suddenly dawned on me that there had been almost no acknowledgment during this whole process of my willingness to compromise to accommodate his dreams. He's the one who wanted kids and it was about to happen only because I agreed to it. Now I was the one pissed off. I let him know that he could at least express some gratitude. I certainly didn't need to be berated for expressing my very valid concerns.

As I mentioned earlier, one of Dustin's most positive attributes is his tenacity. However, that sometimes crosses into tunnel vision when he gets caught up in the process of working toward his goals. So he had lost sight of the fact that at one time I was pretty clear in my fears about parenthood. But he's also one of the sweetest, kindest men you could know. Now that I was finally speaking up and once the initial heat of the moment cooled down, he did take the time to understand my concerns and express his gratitude. Then I realized that his meteoric reaction to my revelations stemmed from his own anxieties.

Things calmed down and we were in good shape when I left town a couple of days later to visit family back East. Thanks to that discussion and my trip, my head was clear by the time I returned a week later. My emotions were now in line with the rest of the parental entourage—excitement and nervous anticipation.

The due date was October 25th and, as the day approached, Daisy definitely looked like she was ready to pop at any moment. Each day at work, Dustin and I felt this build-up of excitement, hoping that the latest ringing of the phone was Daisy calling to let us know that she was in labor. October 25th came and went. Then Halloween arrived and still no kid. The doctor decided that if it didn't come out on its own, they were going to induce. The baby was getting pretty big and could prove a risk to itself or Daisy if it were to get much bigger.

Sure enough, no baby came, so we all checked into the hospital a couple of weeks past the due date. All four members of the parental entourage as well as Daisy's mom were in the delivery room. Daisy had told her mom long before that everyone planned to be there for the delivery and that she was welcome as well. Her mom was a traditional woman. In her day, it was just the mother and medical staff while the father and any others stayed in the waiting room or at home. But she didn't push the matter and chose to be there with us. For much of the initial few hours, she had her face buried in a newspaper as the rest of us were peeking during the exams and asking all sorts of questions. We did catch her curiously peeking around the paper on several occasions, though. Having her there proved to be a tremendous bonding experience, bringing us all closer as we experienced that wonderful night together.

After some poking, prodding and testing, Daisy was given a stimulant to kick-start the labor. Then it was just a matter of waiting. The time ticked away as we talked, read, napped and took turns getting food. Nothing seemed to be happening. The dilatation was minimal even several hours later. It wasn't until after dark that the labor pains began. Daisy was hoping for a meds-free birth and held out for a few hours before finally asking for an epidural, which was administered around midnight. We all slept on and off for the next few hours before Daisy announced that it was time. The nurse was called in, followed by the doctor. Then things really took off.

In short order, the room was filled with several nurses, an attending pediatrician and a resident in training. Daisy's mom stayed at the head of the bed holding her hand, Dustin was propping up her left leg and Daisy's partner and I took turns holding the right leg. It took a while, but then the doctor mentioned seeing the head coming through. To me, it just looked like some grayish-purple internal organ peeking out. Watching the birth was alternatively exciting, emotional and nauseating.

After what seemed like hours and starting to think the doctor might call for a C-section, the baby suddenly slipped out. The first thing that struck me was the eyes. They were wide open and already looking around, as if thinking, *Whoa! This is new*.

Dustin said "It's a boy," one second before the doctor proclaimed, "It's a girl." Dustin thinks it was probably the umbilical cord that confused him. The baby was whisked away to the incubator for clean-up and within seconds, she was letting out the sweetest little cry. Her bottom lip quivered when she did. Whatever doubts I might have had earlier about having kids were instantly gone. Imagine that.

As our baby Teresa lay in the incubator, Dustin and I leaned over her while she held my finger, the whole time staring right into our eyes. To this day, her eyes are still her most striking feature. They are beautifully shaped and the color is a random combination of her mother's blue eyes and my hazel. The result is a kaleidoscopic hue of gold, green, blue and brown. They are also highly expressive and penetrating. Over the years, she's proven to be uncannily perceptive, picking up on people's slightest expressions and shifts in tone of voice.

In addition to learning how to keep an infant alive and unharmed, the next few months were spent establishing a routine for our shared custody. It was pretty simple initially, since we already had determined that the baby was going to live with Daisy full-time for the first year while breastfeeding. As she was weaned, she could start spending nights at our home. The original plan was to begin one night with the dads, then two nights and then eventually alternating one full week at each home. But now that she was born, was that really an ideal schedule?

We decided to enlist the help of a child psychologist who specialized in shared custody cases. The most important aspect of shared custody is what is best for the child. Sure, we might have issues with a certain schedule, but we're the adults and should be able to handle it if the schedule doesn't fit our wants. If it's possible a certain schedule is harmful to the child's development, then that takes precedence over our convenience.

Thanks to the counselor, we learned that in the early years it's actually good to go with shorter splits, since the baby will still be bonding with everyone. And even though we could all see her every day, there are benefits of actually going to sleep and waking up in each home without too many days in between. As kids get older, then longer durations at each home are best.

But probably the most important thing we learned—and the biggest relief—is that growing up in two homes or having four parents is not inherently harmful. Children adapt easily to their routines. Our child was going to grow up with two homes and several parents from the start, so she wouldn't think anything of it. The important factor is that we provide structure and stability within the routines we create. The dads have to be consistent within their home, the moms in theirs and all four when we spend time together. Not that there weren't plenty of other ways for us to screw up our kids, but at least our alternative approach to child-rearing was not a danger.

There were times when this now-living, breathing result of all our planning stirred up unexpected emotions. At times we all felt overly protective, jealous, inadequate or dejected. I can understand why a new child might cause a strain in relationships. Everyone is competing for the affections of a being who can't even control its own bowels, let alone assure us that we're all important to her. It's easy to understand how emotions could escalate so that one parent sees another as a threat to his or her ability to forge the strongest possible bond with a new baby.

Fortunately, the key factor in the success of our family has been the temperaments of all involved. We're a pretty chill group with no outright control freaks or drama queens. We kept our emotions in check and it didn't take long to settle into a routine that reassured us that no one was going to grab the baby and run for the border.

The remainder of the year went by uneventfully. Dustin and I each took some paternity leave from our jobs to spend a few quality weeks with Teresa. Our shared custody schedule eventually settled into the one suggested by our counselor, basically alternating nights at each home.

Then Teresa began daycare. We found the perfect place, both in terms of location and quality. Just a few blocks from our house, a young and recently certified childcare provider was starting up her own daycare business. This was the time when Teresa began interacting with children outside of our own circle of friends. That meant her new friends were going to be exposed to an alternative family for possibly the first time. We wondered how their parents might feel about that. Being in San Jose, it has never been that much of a concern for us. If someone chooses to live in this city, they know to expect diverse cultures and ways of life.

As expected, our four-way, same-sex-couples parenting was a non-issue in the negative sense, but still of great interest. When meeting other parents and explaining how our family works, the reactions tended to be ones of envy above anything else. It seems that many parents love the idea of spreading responsibilities among four adults instead of one or two. Not exactly a major revelation.

But that's San Jose. In the summer of 2008 it was time for all of us to take our first long trip together to the annual reunion of Dustin's family in

Indiana. The entire region is flat for miles in all directions. Small clusters of homes are separated by endless acres of empty fields and farms growing corn and soybeans. We were definitely not in San Jose anymore.

I had already made it to a reunion a few years earlier and I was readily accepted by the extended family without a second thought. Teresa and the baby mamas received an equally warm welcome from the gathering of sixty-plus family members. There was no tension, cold shoulders or veiled expressions of disapproval. If anyone actually did disapprove, we felt none of it.

Teresa's first trip to meet her extended family was a success on another important level: It was the first time we all travelled together across the country. Our dynamics at home adapted well to the road and we all remained calm and collected under pressure. It was the first of several trips over the coming years and, knock on wood, all of them have gone smoothly.

Our next milestone came later in 2008 when, after two previous weddings that were purely symbolic, we were finally legally married at San Jose City Hall. Third time's the charm! Teresa was very excited to be our flower girl and Dustin was holding her in his arms as we said our vows. A month later, she turned two.

As 2009 kicked off, we got around to planning for Teresa's little brother or sister. This time it only took two attempts to conceive. In December 2009, Teresa's sister, Frances, also proved unwilling to make her entry into the world. Once again, the birth needed to be induced two weeks past the due date.

We returned to the child counselor shortly after Frances's birth to perform a status check and were given a positive review. It was a relief to know that we were still on the right track. And having already kept child number one alive for three years now, we were far more confident with number two. In fact, we sometimes felt guilty over how lax we were when compared to the hyper-cautious approach we took with Teresa. Frances didn't receive the same level of germ prevention or safety procedures. In other words, she was treated like most second children.

As her personality has emerged, it's probably just as well that Frances didn't have us doting on her too heavily. She is supremely independent and more than happy to be left alone to entertain herself. She loves to play with her sister when it suits her, but when she wants her alone time, her imagination is company enough. And the way that imagination works, the humor and expressions, it just cracks me up. I often say that my head might explode from her cuteness.

As of this writing, Frances is four and Teresa is seven. Both take swimming classes once a week and Teresa has played both soccer and basketball as part of her school's team. Teresa attends a Catholic School where her gay parents are a non-issue. It's not even an issue that three of her four parents aren't even Catholic; Daisy is the only one. The school fosters a tight-knit community and is welcoming to all. Frances is in the same nursery school that Teresa attended previously and will eventually join her big sister at the same Catholic school. The girls are often the envy of their classmates for having so many parents. The look of wonder on their faces when they meet Teresa or Frances's "other" mom or dad is the sweetest thing.

Our current shared-custody schedule is that the girls spend all Mondays and Tuesdays with the dads and all Wednesdays and Thursdays with the moms. Then we alternate on Fridays through Sundays. This is a common schedule used by divorced parents, according to the child counselor. One of our friends used it successfully with his own son, so we even had a real-world example to go by. However, we also spend a lot of time together as a whole family, regardless of which home the girls will be sleeping at on a given night.

From the very beginning, our agreement was that all major holidays—Thanksgiving, Christmas and Easter—were to be spent together, as well as birthdays. We also take an annual vacation together and smaller weekend getaways. We all participate in school activities and attend sporting events. Other than the separate homes, the girls see their parents as a united front, collectively focused on their well-being. They know we are one family.

A common question we receive is who are the parents under the law and how are the other parents covered legally? For the moms, it is pretty straightforward: Daisy is the full legal parent and her name is on the birth certificate. Meanwhile, her partner has legal documents for guardianship and to act as healthcare proxy.

For Dustin and I, it's a bit more complicated. Since he couldn't be the biological father, it became important to me that Dustin was the legal father. It was originally his dreams that led to the birth of these children, so I wanted him to have a connection to the kids that was more substantial than just "He's dad because we say so."

Here's where it gets a little convoluted.

After the birth, my name was placed on the birth certificate and I filled out a Declaration of Paternity, a document in California that men sign to acknowledge that, yes, they are and want to be the legal father. Then I later signed over my legal rights as father to Dustin so he could adopt the girls, but with a rider on the paperwork that I was guaranteed visitation rights in a worst-case scenario. So Dustin is the legal father via adoption, while my name remains on the birth certificate and declaration of paternity, with the added protections of the adoption rider.

These multiple steps serve more practical purposes than just my sentimental motivations mentioned above. They also clearly establish that Dustin and I are both committed to these children. So in a worst-case scenario, a family court will take everything into consideration and not just turn one or both of us away as never having been a true active parent.

All of this paperwork could also come in handy should there ever be trouble while travelling. We bring along the adoption forms so no one ever questions Dustin's rights, as well as the birth certificates and declaration of paternity so I'm not questioned, either. Granted, my forms are legally moot due to the adoption, but Joe Average doesn't necessarily know that. A birth certificate is a universally-recognized document and the paternity form adds some extra weight. Fingers crossed, it should all be enough to minimize challenges in emergency situations.

In 2013, California passed a law that permits family courts to approve full parenting rights for three or more adults where previously there could only be two. This law doesn't mean a committee of people can just decide to have a kid together and all be equally recognized from day one. But it does give judges the leeway to approve legal recognition of a third parent or more if it is in the best interest of the child. An example of how this is a good thing is a case where a child has an absentee parent and a step-parent is willing to become a full, legal parent. On a case-by-case basis, a judge could approve it. This way, if the legal parent with custody becomes incapacitated or dies, the child doesn't end up in legal limbo due to the absence of the other legal parent. But that's just one scenario. There is also the possibility that with our seven-plus years of established involvement as parents, Daisy's partner and I might be able to petition to be recognized under the law. It's an exciting thought and one we intend to research.

On the more mundane side, our daily routine involves a lot of driving back and forth between the homes, which are about twenty minutes apart. This is the one definite inconvenience about our situation and one we had hoped to rectify by buying a two-unit home together. Unfortunately, the housing market just isn't cooperating. First there was the 2008 crash, which made selling our current homes impossible. And now we're experiencing a real estate boom so insane that, while we can sell our homes, we can't afford to buy a decent new one. And leaving the city isn't an option. We love it here too much.

So, for the time being, the commute is the worst thing we have to deal with. By this point, our cars could probably drive the route on auto-pilot. And while the child counselor we consulted had assured us that the two-home model wasn't detrimental to the girls, it still gives us a twinge of guilt when they sometimes say they wish we all lived together.

I don't mean to make co-parenting sound like all rainbows and unicorns and guaranteed success. There are various factors that need to be present in order for such an unorthodox arrangement to work. The right personalities are probably the most important thing, even above any legal or biological concerns. Selfishness, inability to communicate, lack of self-awareness, the need to control and other negative traits are all potential dangers. But when the right personalities come together—as they have in our case—it can be pretty darn awesome.

Some advantages to co-parenting that are sprinkled throughout our story should be expanded a bit. I'd mentioned the joint bank account we created for the girls' finances. Living in one of the most expensive cities in the country, the financial burden is pretty high, even for those who are child-free. It's a no-brainer that four incomes are better than two. There was a period right as the Great Recession kicked in when both moms lost their jobs. Fortunately, they both found work again within a year, but Teresa and Frances's welfare was never a concern in the meantime.

None of us have any family nearby. They're all back East or in the Midwest. That makes our local support network pretty limited. We know of couples who had children in San Jose and then had to move to where their extended families lived so their parents or siblings could help out. By co-parenting, we have created a support network for ourselves and our children.

All of the above, plus the scheduled nights off from childcare duty to relax and focus on other areas of our lives, removes a lot of the stress that accompanies parenting. That means when the girls are with us we're usually well-rested and able to focus completely on them. However, the key word here is "usually." There are times when life just doesn't care about schedules.

We're not the only ones successfully raising children as intentional co-parents, either. We personally know several others and each family has its own configuration. In our case, it's two couples (two moms and two dads) living in different homes with the kids spending half their time in each. Another family is a mom and a dad, both gay and living in the same house. Another is a straight woman and a gay man living in different homes and yet another is a single gay man and a single lesbian in different homes. There are others out there as well, couples and individuals, all successfully co-parenting.

The concept has even been flirted with on TV. *Grey's Anatomy* and the soap opera *Days of Our Lives* have both had plotlines involving co-parented families, although not necessarily defined as such. The co-parenting in those storylines wasn't by choice, but at least it was instituted from the moment of the child's birth, so it was never presented as anything other than a non-traditional family from the outset. The shows' writers were exposing their audiences to the concept that loving, committed parents don't need to be in love and committed to each other in order to be dedicated and successful parents.

So now, with seven years of being a parent under my belt, have all my past fears been completely put to rest? Well, I'll say that co-parenting was 100 percent the correct decision for us and one I would not change. Our amazing girls have four parents all caring for them, loving them and each sharing the best they have to offer.

For Dustin and I, co-parenting has been an unequivocal success and our daughters are thriving because of it.

# George Tennant

BELFAST, IRELAND

I have always wanted to be a parent. Always. And I kind of always knew that I was going to be one, but paradoxically couldn't imagine how it might happen. The beginning of my journey came in a strange way: My ex-partner told me that his friend Dawn and her partner, Helen, were researching IVF treatment and had been to a clinic, where they realized the cost was too prohibitive, ending their hopes for a child.

I can clearly remember saying, in a very throwaway manner, "Well I have loads of the stuff if they want it." But then after hearing the words aloud and thinking of them, I told my ex-partner to call Dawn and Helen. If they wanted a donor, I was willing to do it. Simple as that. They were both very taken aback. We had met a few times before, but made no real impression on each other. After a few days of consideration, they called me and asked if we could meet.

The first chat was awkward. I can be slow to speak openly and the girls were the opposite—they knew exactly what they wanted. They asked if I wanted to simply donate or have a part in the child's upbringing. I said I was happy to do either. Their preference was for me to have no involvement, but I think they knew I hadn't given the idea the appropriate amount of thought, so I left with a few things to mull over and we planned to meet again.

It was a tough couple of days. I wanted to help Dawn and Helen first and foremost; that was why I hadn't given it much thought in the first place. It just seemed like the good thing to do. I didn't want payment; money was never something I considered. But I also struggled with the idea that my future child was going to live ten minutes away and I wouldn't be able to have any part in her life. Dawn's preference was clear: donate and go. Helen, a few years older, was more open to me being involved. Eventually, I told them what I wanted, which was to be seen as the child's father and to be involved in his or her life.

Dawn was hesitant, but Helen was much happier to consider my wishes. Between the two of them they agreed, so we decided to start straightaway. First they fairly requested that I have an HIV test done. Once that showed clear, it was a short wait until Dawn's fertile time.

I went to their home and deposited into a small jar. Looking back, conceiving was kind of comical at times. They waited in the bedroom with the TV on loud, presumably stifling giggles, while I did my thing in the living room. One time I got carried away and missed the jar. I freaked out and my heart started racing as I frantically tried to clean up my mess and hide the fact my jeans had large wet spots in the crotch and down the leg. I left the jar on the table and ran out the door, hoping to avoid all human contact until I was able to get home so no one would see the evidence of my poor aim.

On days when my aim wasn't an issue, fulfilling my solo duties with Helen and Dawn in the other room still felt awkward. I normally left the jar in the kitchen and rushed out of the house as soon as I was done.

The first cycle didn't work. Neither did the second or third.

This went on for about eight months until one day I finally got the call. Dawn was pregnant, maybe four or five weeks along; several tests said yes. Now things were very, very real! I had to let my parents know. My parents were in their early sixties and had supported me in everything I ever did. Honestly, I couldn't ask for better, but I was still terrified to tell them. There were no gay parents anywhere to be seen in my parents' circle or even the media. This was going to come as a shock.

I was shaking, but it had to be done. I sat them both down and said I had some news I wanted to discuss. I was going to be a dad with two lesbians. They thought I was joking. I eventually got it through to them, but they were still bewildered. I said I was going to let the news sink in and drop by in the next couple of days so we could discuss it again.

However, the next day I got a call from Helen. Dawn had lost the baby that night. I was devastated, as were they. So I called my parents back, this time with the bad news. They were saddened. They had come around to the idea a lot quicker than I thought.

Dawn, Helen and I took a month off and then got back to trying the following month. However, things began to change between us. To be honest, the miscarriage shook me more than I expected and I lost some of my enthusiasm. It went on like this for several months, but one time I made an excuse not to go over. Another time, they did. Then they said they wanted to rethink the whole thing. We met a couple of months later and they said they'd changed their minds.

At that stage, I had become fed up with the monthly chore of depositing and I'm sure they picked up on that, which may have made me look like a less attractive option as a father. Our friendship was also waning. But I could see the pain in their faces, so the pleaser in me offered to just be a donor again and nothing more if that's what they wanted. They did, so we all agreed to start again, with me prepared to bow out when the pregnancy occurred. So again, months of trying ensued. I had a sperm count check and was ridiculously proud to hear I had an above-average count. Dawn had some tests too, all of which were fine.

Next, we went to a clinic to see if they could help. But they didn't treat single women and especially not people of our persuasion. So Dawn and I pretended to be in a relationship. We held hands and tried to act like a committed, happy couple while Helen hid outside in the car. It worked. We convinced them. The doctor gave Dawn a pack of tablets and off we went. The second month in, I got the call: Dawn was pregnant again.

Instead of being elated, I was upset. I wasn't going to be a father, but they were going to be mothers. The call was them giving me their news, not telling me mine. They invited me over for dinner to say thanks. I went, but couldn't hide my feelings. During dinner, Helen asked if I wanted involvement or if I wanted to stick to my previous plan. It was time to be honest and nothing less. So I was. I told them I wanted this child the same as they did. It was awkward and unpleasant, so I left shortly after.

At our next meeting, it was evident that Dawn wasn't happy with my change of plans, although Helen seemed accepting at best. We decided to put my name on the child's birth certificate and let Dawn and Helen choose a first name. Dawn had changed her family name to Helen's, so the baby's last name was already determined. They agreed to go over future decisions with me, but they ultimately had the final say on everything. Contact frequency was promised not to be an issue. Only Helen was allowed to be present during birth, but I could visit the hospital.

I thought all of these were fair decisions. But as the pregnancy progressed, I began to feel excluded, unwanted and uncomfortable. I told my family and friends about the impending birth and they were all pleased and supportive, excited even. I went through a whole range of emotions during that time. I found it difficult to tell my straight friends, who had trouble conceiving that I was going to be a parent. They were obviously happy for me, but who could blame them for any other feelings they might have had? One friend even wanted to know if my child was more likely to be gay.

The girls and I arranged to meet for coffee one day about five months into the pregnancy. We had exchanged texts and e-mails, but the need for constant contact was no longer there. They informed me their plans had changed. I was no longer going to be included on the birth certificate. This ensured that whatever limited rights I may have had were eliminated completely. I wasn't going to be welcomed at the hospital and any contact for the first year was restricted to me visiting the child in their home. I felt angry and pushed out. They had gotten what they wanted and now they wanted me gone.

It made me think of how I'd changed my own mind for them. I reminded them that the baby was only here because of my help and said I couldn't go along with this reduced role. They told me this was how it was going to be—take it or leave it. Ultimately, I left it. I felt forced into a corner and I believed that if I had accepted this new arrangement, there was going to be another list of changes later on designed to move me even further out of my child's life. It broke my heart and I went home that night and cried myself to sleep. But it had happened and now I had to deal with it.

We met again by accident when Dawn was seven or eight months along. At that point, we had no choice but to go for coffee and tie up loose ends. Old ground was gone over; nothing had changed and neither had anyone's stance. I wished them the best and they promised to let me know when the baby was born and send me a photograph.

True to their word, once my daughter was born in early 2005, they sent me some photos. They named her Alison. I told my family, who didn't really know how to react. In truth, I was elated. But the following nine months were to be the most stressful and difficult of all my thirty-eight years. I ended up ruining the job I had and was unable to look at babies who were my child's age. Also, as the girls and I lived near each other, I was apprehensive about going anywhere local in case I ran into them.

Christmas approached and that's when I made a decision. While I may not have had any contact with Alison then, I fully expected that to change when she was old enough to ask questions. I wanted the chance to show her that she was in my thoughts, so I got a decent-sized sum of money together and a card wishing them a happy Christmas and apologizing for anything I had done. On December 22nd, I dropped it into their postbox. The money was to provide Alison with some Christmas presents from me, but I assured Dawn and Helen that they didn't have to let her know where the presents came from. I planned to do this each birthday and Christmas with no expectations. The next day, I found a card dropped into my postbox with a photo, a thank you note and the following invitation: "Do you want to come over on Christmas Eve to meet Alison?"

I was overwhelmed with joy and shock. Sure enough, on December 24th, I was there. The girls were friendly and a little nervous. At nine months, Alison was a happy, smiley little baby. I remember her climbing onto my knee and Helen taking a photo, which I still cherish. Then Helen asked if I wanted to come back again after Christmas. Easy question! I said, "Yes, of course I would."

Then the next question: "George, do you want to be involved in her life?"

I can still feel that moment. The next day was Christmas. As always, I had dinner with my folks. After the meal, I took out the photo that Dawn and Helen had given me and told my parents about the previous day, how I was now going to have contact with my daughter and they with their grandchild. Wow, the happiness we all felt that day!

A few practicalities had to be discussed. It was clear that Helen was happier to have me involved than Dawn was, but arrangements for finances, contact and such were agreed upon by all. Then I became Alison's dad. Since then, Christmas Eve has always been extra special for me, almost like her unofficial birthday.

Alison and I bonded straightaway. She was a joyful child—clever enough to cry when I took her from her mothers and to stop as soon as they were out of earshot. Dawn called or texted me incessantly to check up on her. Often she checked in at least once an hour. Usually, the first call came within five minutes to see how things were going. It was a little irritating, but I had to accept it and anything else that was asked of me, because in truth I was very grateful and also knew who the boss was in this whole arrangement.

Eventually, I picked up on some hints that Dawn and Helen were not getting on as well as they used to. Dawn could be snappy and often rude to Helen, who was always friendlier and more accepting of me. Sometimes I assumed that was the cause of the shift I now saw in their relationship.

But Alison and I loved being together. We talked and talked and sang and sang. We were never quiet. Getting used to early mornings was a trial for me. There were a few times when it got to 6:00 P.M. and I realized I had forgotten to eat, because we were having so much fun that I lost track of time. Her mothers often collected her at 6:00 P.M. and then I was in bed for a snooze within minutes!

I was a relatively self-conscious man and wondered if I could loosen up enough to walk through a mall while baby talking and cooing into the pushchair. But I could. I wanted Alison to be happy and did many things that made me look rather dumb in order to make her laugh or to soothe her and I never cared what anyone else thought.

One day, when Alison was about two and a half, I went to collect her from her home. Dawn was a little anxious and asked me if I had heard from Helen. I told her I hadn't and took Alison out. When I returned, Dawn asked to talk with me. She and Helen had been arguing the previous morning. They had decided the relationship wasn't working and, within the argument, agreed to split. Helen had left, hadn't shown up at work and wasn't answering her phone. Dawn was worried. She called Helen's parents, but they hadn't heard from her either. Neither had Helen's close friends. So Dawn called the police. I stayed with Alison while Dawn went to the police station.

The next day there was still no news until 4:10 P.M. when I received a call from Dawn. A body had been found and she was asked to identify it. The identification on the body belonged to Helen. I needed to leave work and take Alison from her child minder until Dawn got back.

I won't go into detail about that day, because it's not my story to tell. The body was indeed Helen's. There were both signs of suicide and signs that it wasn't intentional. Dawn told Alison on the day of the funeral, but the little girl didn't really understand. A few days later, we were all in my car when Alison asked for her mum again. Dawn explained that her mum had gone to heaven and could see us, but we couldn't see her. The cry from Alison then made us stop the car. She understood at that point and her grieving started.

Helen's death kicked off a completely new stage of the relationship between me and Dawn—and to an extent, me and Alison. For Dawn to come to terms with her grief, she needed more support. Because she was a private person by nature, with not many friends, I became somewhat of a confidante in the immediate aftermath. I also had to take Alison more, which was no problem for me.

The following few years were typified by the fun, love and joy shared between my daughter and me, as well as periods of barely speaking interspersed with rare moments of friendship between Dawn and me. We took Alison out together when possible, which she loved. Dawn didn't have any serious relationships in the meantime and when Alison was four, I met Antonio, a twenty-eight-year-old Brazilian who had been in Ireland for a year.

Alison was told just before this that her family unit was different from others, but no less special, and that she was no different and no less loved by everyone. She was told her parents were gay, which means boys like boys and girls like girls. She wasn't going to know many people who were gay and probably wasn't gay herself, but either way was fine. (The number of One Direction posters in her bedroom now tends to make me think she will be into boys.)

I had been dating Antonio for about a month and we both knew it was the beginning of something serious. I kept Dawn in the loop and planned a very low-key way to have Alison and Antonio meet, which Dawn thought was a good idea. So one day while I had Alison with me, we went to Antonio's home to collect him and drive him to work. Alison was full of chat and questions for him. They talked about Disney princesses and he asked her if she liked "White Snow." She nearly lost her lunch laughing at him and enjoyed correcting him. From then on, all Disney Princesses were renamed with backwards names: Ella-Cinder, Punzel-Rap, Beauty Sleeping...

The next meeting we went for lunch. When I wasn't looking, Antonio dared Alison to put salt in my tea. Oh she loved that! I drank it and almost choked. They high-fived and celebrated; they had gotten me. And they got each other. Later, she asked me, "Dad, is Antonio your boyfriend?"

"How would you feel if he was?" I stuttered.

"I'd feel good, Daddy. You shouldn't be alone." Those are the kinds of moments that stay with you and Alison has always been wise beyond her years.

A couple of weekends away together and many, many cups of tea and salt later, we began to feel like a family. On one of our weekends away, Alison was a little moody and cranky with Antonio, so I took her for a walk. I asked her what was wrong. She has never held back with her thoughts and feelings.

She said, "You have *him* now and you're going to want to have other kids with him and you won't want me." I sat her down and told her that no matter what, she was my number one and Antonio always knew his job was to be number two. And if we did ever have kids, they were going to be from Antonio, so no one was ever going to take her place. She smiled a smile that can only be described as relief. I recounted this to Antonio later and made a point of calling them by their numbers for the rest of the weekend to put her mind at ease.

In 2010, the Republic of Ireland government had agreed to the Civil Partnership law in principle, but hadn't set a timeframe for its introduction. In Northern Ireland, as part of Great Britain, civil partnerships have been legalised since 2005. Since Antonio's immigration status meant his right to stay in the country was not guaranteed and his employment prospects were severely limited, we decided to have a civil partnership in Northern Ireland and wait for the law to catch up in the South.

So in August 2010, we had the most amazing day with family, friends and our flower girl and guest of honour, Alison. When it was time to exchange rings, we also had our best man put a ring on her finger, for her to mark how we were all being united that day. The three of us went on honeymoon to a wildlife and theme park in England.

Antonio is always happy to tell us of a dream he had when he was considering leaving Brazil to move to Ireland. He dreamt that he was on a bridge and a figure in white appeared and told him, "If you cross the bridge and go to Ireland, you will meet a man with a daughter and you will be forever happy. If you don't cross the bridge, your life may not give you this." On the way to the ceremony, we went over a new bridge and he is adamant that it's the one from his dream.

I now have Alison over five nights every two weeks. Her two best friends live beside me, their families happy for all three girls to play at our home or Alison to play at theirs. Sleepovers happen, parties happen, life happens.

Our story ultimately has a happy ending. Dawn and I are, at worst, cordial. On good days, which there are increasingly more of, we're even friendly. I did a radio interview about being a gay parent and she happened to hear it. I was honest in the interview and recounted some of the experiences I have written about here. She said she had no idea I felt the way I did and that she finally saw the affection, love and joy I feel for and receive from my daughter.

Dawn has tried to be friendlier since and, to be fair to her, she has given me a lot more respect than ever before. She's had a tougher break than anyone I know and is unquestionably an outstanding parent. It was never an easy path for either of us, but we do not let that affect how Alison is raised. We work together now much better than we ever have done. We both respect that the other is doing their best.

Alison is the most compassionate child you'll ever see. Her teacher once told me that she had to scold Alison for not sitting in her seat during the lesson and promised a visit to the headmaster if she left her seat again.

Five minutes later, another child started to cry and Alison went right over to her. The teacher told Alison to sit back down.

Alison said, "No, Ella is crying. I'm giving her a hug. When she's okay, I'll sit back down. It's okay. I know I'll be in trouble, but I don't mind." The teacher said it took her aback and that compassion at the risk of trouble was something that couldn't be taught. Alison knows her family is different. So anyone who is in any way different is a friend for her. As she says, we are all different, so we are all the same.

For anyone considering co-parenting, my advice is to make sure you know what you want, what areas can be reconsidered and what won't be. Have everything agreed upon with a lawyer. Be prepared for your relationship with your co-parent to change, because it will. The more you discuss and agree in advance, the better. What happens if one of the couples separates? If one loses a job? If one wants to move from the area? Life is fluid and you simply don't know where it will take you, but you may be taken in a different direction than you planned.

For Antonio, Alison and me, our family is our life. It's where we are happiest. Sometimes, we don't appreciate what we have often enough. Sometimes our friends just don't get how we don't want the lives they have or the ones we used to have. Our journey to being the family we are was not easy, but it has been worth every bit of blood, sweat and tears.

Yours could be too.

# Epilogue
## by Gabriel Blau
Former Executive Director of the Family Equality Council

From the moment I started dating in college, I assumed that, like my parents, I was going to have three children. I planned to have them all before I turned thirty. They would be perfect. My husband would be perfect, too.

When I met my husband, we were in our early twenties. So far, so good. On our first date we talked about commitment, marriage and children. Check. Check. Check. A few years later, after moving in, getting married (before God and community—the state refused to be part of it) and with all the enthusiasm and excitement of a young couple who were going to pursue their dreams without hesitation, we found ourselves at an event in Manhattan hearing about the ways we could become parents through adoption. It was then that we hesitated.

We had to have a child. We had to become parents. We can't explain it, but when my husband and I were in our mid-twenties, we just knew it was time. We were younger than we felt. We were at the beginning of our careers. But we were gay. Gay men in their twenties just didn't do that. They didn't have kids or worry about babysitters and school and college funds. Who were we to challenge that? We were parents without a child, that's who. Today, our child is in the other room, reading a book. I have a PTA meeting tonight. The dishes still need to be washed.

For us, the path was adoption. We just always knew we were going to adopt. There's really no rhyme or reason. People will tell you they had reasons—and they do—as to why they went one direction or another. But the truth is, it all comes down to something mysterious that happens deep inside.

There wasn't a book quite like this when we were deciding to have children. And the world in which we were making that decision was very different from the world today, even though it was less than a decade ago. So it was up to us to figure it out. And therein lies one of the blessings of becoming a parent as an LGBTQ person. We begin from a place of questions. In almost all cases, we must begin from a place of careful consideration and planning. Very few of us have the option of opening a bottle of wine, lighting some candles, not using protection and seeing where the night will take us, unless your idea of a romantic evening is writing checks to attorneys, signing papers, getting fingerprinted and inviting a social worker into your home.

It might not be a "let's see what happens" romantic evening, but there is still magic in this process. Whatever you read in these pages, whatever lists you make to help you figure out your path, whatever advice you get, don't believe for a second it won't be magical. The biggest secret is that jumping through hoops and speaking to surrogates, birthmothers, sperm banks and attorneys doesn't actually diminish the experience. The more I travel the country and listen to parents, the more I realize that all of these processes only enhance our experiences. They have their own magic. The stumbling blocks, the different options, it all somehow comes together in the end and when you are holding your child, you know it had to happen that way. It just had to or your family wouldn't be who they are. With your own journey, your story, you are joining many overlapping communities of LGBTQ parents who have as many origin stories as they have children. We are the most diverse and most intentional family demographic in history.

It may be hard to imagine, but there was a time, not too long ago, where just the simple fact of being LGBTQ meant the courts automatically considered you an unfit parent. As I write this in 2015, there are still courts and legislators that believe we should be denied parental rights. People in our community have been literally torn away from their families and forbidden to have relationships with their children. Over the last few decades, our community has steadily obtained more and more protections for LGBTQ people and their families, but we still have a long way to go until we reach full equality.

By the time you read this, we may have other protections for our families: protections against housing and employment discrimination, protections against discrimination in a restaurant or business. We may even have access to all the legal tools we need to secure our families (second-parent adoption, anyone?), but we'll still need community. The Family Equality Council has been around for over thirty years and every survey they have conducted tells us the same thing: that above all else, there is tremendous power in being together. Your journey will be unique, but along the way you'll meet your community and you'll find that millions of us are there with you.

So what's next? Take a deep breath. Let it out. Appreciate that you are stepping into a journey the likes of which you cannot even imagine. Embrace the confusion and the hard moments, because that's your family story. And one day it's going to be your children's story, the one they will ask you to tell again on their birthdays or the one you may be telling your grandchildren about their parents. So hold tight, take one step at a time and don't forget that you are not alone.

# Words of Advice

**N**ow that you've read this book, I hope that you have a better understanding of the different family-building options available and a good idea of what it's like to actually go through the various journeys. These stories should help you balance the information you receive from agencies to help ensure you have a more complete picture.

Now, to help you move forward with your own family planning, I thought it best to compile some words of advice and encouragement from same-sex parents who have already been through the family-building journey. What did they learn from their experiences and what do they think you should know before embarking on your own journey? Remember to keep in mind that while there may be similarities with different people's experiences, every path is unique and no two stories are the same.

> "The red tape is frustrating and discouraging, but don't give up. The rewards are ten-fold. Stay on top of the process, ask questions or bring to light anything that doesn't seem right. Follow up on everything and assume nothing will get done without that follow-up. Be kind: The social workers and family specialists are underfunded and overworked. Help them and you will be rewarded with a great support system and maybe even a few new friends!"
>
> —Van Welborn (Phoenix, Arizona)

"You don't need to wait for everything to be perfect before you have a child and I honestly wish we had started earlier. We didn't think we were ready financially, so we put it off a few years. In retrospect, that was silly. Also, be patient. It takes a long time and you have to be committed to the process, but it's really worth it!"

      —Demetri Moshoyannis (San Francisco, California)

"Make sure you fully understand the legal costs up front and ask if there are any other expenses that are not included in your fee description. Our lawyer told us that our cost would be $3,000 to $4,000 and it ended up costing us $11,000! Also, do plenty of research to make sure you understand the laws in your state. Read! Read! Read!"

      —Joshua Hampshire (Dallas, Texas)

"I wish we had known more about the process of getting us both recognized as legal parents. Because gay people couldn't adopt together in our state, we had to do two separate adoptions, doubling the expense and the time. Make sure you understand the laws in your state up front. Everything you have to go through is worth it in the end, though. The rewards are endless. Don't rule out older kids or special needs kids, either. They need love just like everyone else."

      —David Angevine (Cleveland, Tennesee)

"We noticed that agencies sometimes omit vital facts about a child in foster care or will even be directly dishonest about a child's behaviors/background in an effort to rapidly, rather than appropriately, place a child. Don't be swayed by emotional pleas from the agency if your gut tells you no. Also, be patient. Don't make enemies of social workers, Court Appointed Special Advocates (CASA), attorneys or others.

When it comes time to advocate for your child—and there will be hundreds of times you will—these people need to work for you and they won't unless you always approach with a smile, even a disingenuous one."

—Thomas Woolley (Fresno, California)

"Don't be discouraged by all the hoops you have to jump through. Stick with it! It can seem like hard work and a lot of paperwork at the time, but it is so worth it in the end! Also, if you're adopting a child who isn't a newborn, don't expect him or her to be immediately well-behaved and fall in line with your values. They will need time and consideration while they learn to be the kind of mini-person you want them to be."

—Vanessa Ingley-Buxton (Derbyshire, United Kingdom)

"I recommend seeing a therapist during the whole process, for both the surrogate and the couple. We had a surrogacy scenario where my partner's best friend offered to donate the eggs and be the carrier. At the end of the third trimester, there were so many emotions and hormones going on, we were all on edge. Having someone there for us as a couple and also for our surrogate was key in our situation."

—Joseph Adelantar (Jersey City, New Jersey)

"Discrimination by doctors and their staff is something that happens. It's important to screen for doctors before you become pregnant. Discrimination from a doctor who is treating you or your partner can not only cost you your dignity and sanity, but can also cost you monetarily as well. Also, don't be afraid to tell people that your reproductive journey is private. Some people think that, just because we have to conceive via a donor, they can ask all of these inappropriate questions. Your journey to parenthood is just that: it's yours. You are not responsible for the education of the ignorant unless you choose to be."

—Amanda Victorian (Lake Charles, Louisiana)

"Sharing your story with those who support you can bring you much joy and create community. Seek out other parents whose experiences are in some ways similar to yours. Tell your stories to them, on your own blog or wherever folks will support you in being the best family you can be without judgment. Also, carry copies of your family documents with you—birth certificates, marriage licenses, adoption records, etc. It's a sad reality that you may encounter officials at car rental counters or emergency rooms who don't recognize you as a family."

—Lisa Haefele-Thomas (Berkeley, California)

"Be prepared to move goalposts. You set out with an idealised plan of how you will form your family, but often numerous factors will affect this, like views on how you'll get pregnant, choice of donor and belief in your own fertility. Each 'change' or difference may require a shift of the original plan but, like your birth plan, flexibility is key. Also, keep in mind that having children makes your relationship more visible. When you have children, right from the beginning of the process, you are forever telling people you are a couple. When people ask 'Whose children are these?' or 'Which one is the Mum?' your answers need to be genuine and honest—your child will hear!"

—Helen (Oxford, United Kingdom)

"Don't get too hung up on your openness plan, because your perspective—and your birthmother's perspective—will likely change post-placement. Just know that after you bring your son or daughter home, you will likely want more contact with the birthmother than you thought you would; your birth-mother may want less than she thought she did and contact can change over time. Knowing that contact might drop off, be sure to write down your child's birthfamily details—don't rely on memory. Our kids are now one and four and we think about their birthmothers constantly."

—Ian Hart (San Francisco, California)

"Talk about it with people you trust. If you are using a known donor, work out exactly what you are wanting from that person (contact, pictures, personal info) and draw up a contract so that it is in black and white. This will help ensure everyone is on the same page. Be totally upfront and honest and think very carefully about using a donor whom you know. We tried this and things got very awkward. Take your time and don't rush into any decision. It has to be right for all parties involved. Also, enjoy trying for a baby; it is not a chore. Enjoy every moment, because it is an amazing journey."

—Shelley Jenkins (Gloucestershire, United Kingdom)

"Discuss all expectations in advance, no matter how uncom-fortable: religion, approach to discipline, whether or not to circumcise, legal custody, etc. Also, be ready to call it off. Whether bringing a new life into the world or a child into your home via adoption, this is serious stuff. Once that baby is around there's no turning back. If there are red flags flying beyond the anxiety that is to be expected, then be ready to put things on hold. One of the advantages for prospective LGBT parents is that we can take our time.

— Bill Delaney (San Francisco, California)

# Wrapping Things Up

Adoption, fostering, surrogacy, assisted reproduction and co-parenting are all ways in which LGBT couples can begin the journey of building their family. Each road is unique and it's important for you to choose the path that best fits your family.

There are many challenges to becoming a parent outside of a heterosexual relationship and you will undoubtedly encounter numerous ups and downs along the way. Your journey could be stressful, emotional and frustrating and at times you may feel hopeless, but remember there is a light at the end of the tunnel.

Nothing can prepare you for that moment when you first hold your child in your arms. When you do, you'll find yourself in a blissful bubble. Nothing else will matter in that moment and, down the road, you'll tell yourself that everything you went through was worth it in the end.

If you've already started the journey and you find yourself going through a challenging time, just remember that as long as you have the patience and perseverance to withstand the emotional rollercoaster of the journey, you can eventually have a happy family of your own (white picket fence optional).

# Acknowledgments

You know the phrase, "It takes a village?" Well, that's definitely the case with this book. So many people helped with this project and I couldn't have finished it without them. I want to take the opportunity to give a shout out to some of the people who helped in a big way.

First and foremost, thank you to my agent, Chelsea Lindman, for believing in my manuscript and me when so many others didn't. I appreciate the guidance and suggestions you provided. None of this would have been possible without you and for that, I am forever grateful.

My amazing husband, Mat Rosswood, thank you for your patience and for the days that you spent helping me weed through all the story submissions.

Mom, thank you for helping with babysitting while I went through my final edits. I couldn't have gotten through crunch time without you!

Melissa Gilbert, I am truly honored that you helped with this project. You have a beautiful soul and a big heart. Thank you for being a vocal advocate and an amazing ally.

Charlie Condou, thank you for being a positive role model for other LGBT parents. You have helped so many people by living your life openly. I appreciate you taking the time to share your story with me and for being one of the first people who stepped up and offered to help with this project!

Samantha LemMon, thank you for the awesome book cover and for being extremely patient with me as we went through a gazillion versions!

Beki Eckles Andreasen, thanks for the great headshots. You are the only one who can get me to wear a sweater in the dead heat of summer in San Diego!

Kate Kendell, Cathy Sakimura and the team at NCLR, thank you for your edits, tips and legal advice! When I needed help, you were more than happy to step up and I appreciate it.

John F. Stephens, thanks for all your guidance with navigating the copyright issues and release forms. I don't know what I would have done without you!

Gabriel Blau, thank you for everything you do to help LGBT families. I am extremely grateful you shared your expertise with me and wrote the wonderful epilogue for this book. I look forward to working together in the future.

Ian Hart and Nick Larocque, I learned so much from the two of you! Thank you for sharing your family-building experiences with Mat and I, and for being such great mentors.

Judy Appel, Renata Moreira, Yusni Bakar and the rest of the team at Our Family Coalition, thank you for helping me collect stories for this project and for helping to create a local community of families like ours.

Ben Barr, Julianne Carroll, Wade Meyer and the team at the Rainbow Community Center, you helped build a network of local LGBT families and put me in touch with some amazing people!

Joe Jasko, JoAnne Thomas, Charley Nasta and the folks at New Horizon Press, thank you for all the hard work you put in behind the scenes. You helped polish everything up and made it presentable. You were so helpful and I appreciate the fact that you were willing to work with me. Thank you for being such great partners. I'm so happy you were on my team!

Dr. Joan S. Dunphy, you helped so many families when you agreed to take on this project. I only wish you were still here to see all the smiles you helped create.

And finally, thank you to everyone who contributed by sharing his or her personal story. You helped create something special. When people read this book, I hope they feel like they are going to a trusted friend for advice, someone who has been through the journey before. You are that friend and by sharing your emotional and raw experience, you have made the journey to parenthood a little easier for someone else.

# Legal Considerations

*(provided by the National Center for Lesbian Rights)*

Please note that family law is very complex and differs state by state. Also, what's common or legal in this country may not be common or legal in another country. You may even have to abide by the laws of multiple regions if the various parties involved reside in different locations. It is highly recommended that you speak with an experienced attorney in LGBT family law. The National Center for Lesbian Rights was extremely helpful when it came to answering my questions and they even provided a list of legal issues to consider for each section of this book. I recommend contacting them if you need more information about the laws in your state or if you need information about attorneys in your area. You can find them at www.nclrights.org/gethelp.

## General

When you decide to bring children into your home, it is very important to think about how your family will be legally protected. Make sure you know the answers to these questions before you get started:

- Will I be recognized as a parent under the law in my state? Will my spouse or partner be recognized as a parent too?

- Will the genetic or birthparents—including a sperm or egg donor, surrogate or birthmother—have parental rights and is it possible to terminate those rights?
- If I am adopting, what are the laws in my state about adoption? Can I adopt? Can my partner and I adopt together if we are not married?

## Adoption

For people who live in the United States, here are a few key points to keep in mind if you are considering adoption. If you have legal questions or concerns after reading this section, it is best to consult a lawyer for legal advice.

- Some states allow unmarried couples to adopt jointly, but not all do.
- All states allow married spouses to adopt jointly, from an agency, private placement or foster care.
- If the birthparents' rights are not properly protected, your adoptions can become more costly and you may even end up losing your child. If you are adopting from an agency, you should ask questions about what has been done to ensure that the birthparents' rights have been properly protected in the way that the law in your state requires.

## Foster Care

For those living in the United States, here are a few key points to keep in mind if you are considering foster care. If you have legal questions or concerns, you should consult an attorney for legal advice.

- In nearly every state, a person with an unmarried partner can foster a child. Consult with a lawyer if you have questions on whether or not your state allows this.
- All states allow married couples and single individuals to be foster parents.

# Surrogacy

The legal requirements for surrogacy in the United States are very specific. It is vital that you consult with a knowledgeable attorney before entering any surrogacy agreement.

- The laws about surrogacy are very different in different states. In some states, surrogacy is illegal and many states provide no protections for families using surrogacy. States that do allow surrogacy have specific rules you have to follow.

- Every state that protects families using surrogacy requires the gestational method, where the egg donor is different from the gestational carrier.

- If you are thinking about going to another country for surrogacy, consider the potential emotional and financial cost if you run into complications. Depending on your situation, you may not be able to bring your baby back to the United States or you may have lengthy delays before you can return. International surrogacy is complex and doesn't have clear protections.

- If you conceive through surrogacy, it is important to get a court judgment recognizing you as a parent. You can also do an adoption to make sure your parental rights have been established.

# Assisted Reproduction

It is highly recommended that you speak to a lawyer experienced in assisted reproduction law before you start trying to become pregnant. Here are a few important legal issues of which you should be aware if you are considering assisted reproduction in the United States:

- If you are using a known sperm or egg donor, it is important to know that not all states protect families using donors to conceive. Some states do have these laws, but they are limited to married couples or they apply only to people who have conceived with the assistance of a doctor. If your state doesn't have donor laws or you do not follow the donor laws in your state, your known donor may be a legal parent until you terminate your donor's rights with an adoption. A written agreement by itself will not terminate your donor's parental rights, even if that is what it says. However, it is still important to have a written agreement, because it can be used as evidence if you end up in a legal challenge.

- If you are an intended single parent using a known donor, it is vital that you are sure you are protected by a donor law in your state. In most states, if your donor is or may be a parent, there is no way to terminate your donor's parental rights unless another second parent adopts.

- If one of you is giving birth and you are married or in a civil union or comprehensive domestic partnership, you should both be able to be on the birth certificate. However, being on the birth certificate does not necessarily make you a parent. You have to know whether there is a law that protects you as such.

- It is strongly recommended that all non-biological parents get an adoption or court judgment of parentage if possible, even if you are married. This ensures that your parental rights are protected in any state, no matter where you travel or move.

## Co-Parenting

Here are a few key points to keep in mind if you are considering entering into a co-parenting arrangement in the United States. If you have legal questions or concerns after reading this section, it is best to consult a lawyer.

- If you are co-parenting with another person and you both will be the biological parents, you should both be able to be on the birth certificate and recognized as parents under the law. Every state has a system where an unmarried birthmother and the biological father can sign and file a form acknowledging that he is the biological father.

You need to make sure that you follow the procedures required by your state.

- If one or both co-parents are not biological or birthparents, you should find out how your state treats non-biological parents before conceiving. In some states, an unmarried second parent of a child conceived through assisted reproduction can be legally recognized if they consent to the assisted reproduction in writing. In some states, a non-biological and non-birthparent may need to do a second-parent adoption in order to be legally recognized. However, not all states allow unmarried people to do second-parent adoptions. In some states, you may not be able to protect an unmarried non-biological parent's rights.

- If you are co-parenting with more than one other parent, only a few states acknowledge that a child can have more than two legally recognized parents. However, you may be able to do a third-parent adoption in some states.

# Reasons Why and Challenges

## Reasons Why People Choose **Open Adoption**

**The opportunity to meet your child's biological parents** – When you choose open adoption, you have the opportunity to meet your child's birthmother (and possibly the birthfather if he is still in the picture).

**Family connection** – Adoptees who don't have the benefit of knowing their adoption story can end up fantasizing about their biological family. The search for answers can be exhausting, both emotionally and financially. However, children of open adoption have this information available to them from the beginning. Because of this, it is less likely that your child will need to search for or fantasize about his or her birthfamily.

**The opportunity to be present during birth** – Once you have met a birthmother and everyone decides to match and move forward together, you will most likely create what is referred to as a birth plan. This is where you decide who will be present during the birth, who holds the baby first, who cuts the umbilical cord and more. If you match early enough and the birthmother agrees, you may even have the opportunity to be in the same room during birth if that is something you want.

**Raising a child from birth** – For some people, being involved in a child's life on day one is important to them. This allows them to witness key developmental milestones such as seeing their baby's first smile, hearing their child's first words or watching them take their first step.

**Access to medical information** – Medical background information can be vital when it comes to making informed medical decisions. You will likely have this information for your child in the beginning and if there are any health changes to your child's biological family in the future, you may have the opportunity to receive that information as well. Please note that sometimes the birthfather is unknown or no longer in the picture and in situations like that, you may not have medical information from the birthfather's side of the family.

**Answers to difficult questions** – If you remain in contact with your child's birthparents, they may be able to help you answer difficult questions from your child such as, "Why did my birthparents place me for adoption?" Your son or daughter may have the opportunity to hear the answers straight from his or her birthparents.

**Support** – Becoming a parent can be a stressful journey. If you work with an open adoption agency, you will likely have emotional support to help you get through the challenges that pop up along the way. The support could come in the form of a counselor or support group filled with other families in the same situation as you, sharing their experiences with each other.

## Open Adoption Challenges

**Unpredictable waiting periods** – Once you have been approved and have completed your birthmother letter, you pretty much have to sit and wait for a birthmother to contact you. There's no telling how long that can take. You could be contacted as soon as you get approved or you could wind up waiting three years! The lack of control and unknown future can be very stressful and may even take a toll on your relationship with your partner. Open communication and support for each other is key here.

**Emotional stress** – There are many things that will cause stress during the adoption process. Completing mounds of paperwork, going through background checks, getting medical exams and having a home study are just the beginning. It is common for people to worry about why it's taking so long for them to get chosen. Once they do get chosen, they may feel a need to keep their guard up in fear of saying or doing something that could make the birthmother decide to choose another couple. The constant doubt can be exhausting and draining.

**Scams** – The adoption journey is an emotional one and unfortunately there are people who use this as an opportunity to prey on prospective parents. Some scams are financially motivated, while others are just about someone wanting to mess with your head. Adoption agencies can help weed out potential scams, but there is no guarantee you will not encounter one.

**Possibility that a match will fall through** – There is no guarantee that a match with a potential birthmother will result in placement. There are many reasons why a match could fall through: The birthmother could change her mind, a relative may step in to help raise the child or something else could happen that changes the circumstances of the situation. The benefit of working with an open adoption agency is that they do thorough intakes with birthparents to assess their situation and help them make the right decision for them. Because of these intakes, when you work with a reputable agency the risks of a birthmother backing out are minimized.

## Reasons Why People Choose **Foster Care**

**Lots of support** – When you become a foster parent, you will have numerous resources available to help you along the way. Support is offered to help you adjust to becoming a foster parent and it is also offered throughout your journey.

**Helping others** – When you become a foster parent, you are helping a child who has nowhere else to go. There are many reasons why children go into foster care: They may have come from abusive homes or they may have lost their parents. When you open your home to a foster child, you'll not only be helping them, but you'll be helping families and whole communities as well.

**Economical** – When adopting a child through foster care, you won't have the hefty fees associated with surrogacy or private adoption. Foster parents may also receive a monthly stipend to help feed, clothe and meet the basic needs of the children placed in their care. While money should never be a reason to become a foster parent, it does help with taking care of a child.

**Helping young people in the LGBT community** – Unfortunately, there are still kids who get kicked out of their homes because of their sexual orientation or gender identity and it can be hard for LGBT children in foster care to find permanent homes. It can also be hard to find people willing to take in a child with HIV/AIDS. As an LGBT parent, you are in a unique position to help kids in our community grow up in a safe, stable and accepting environment.

## Foster Care Challenges

**Possible separation** – One of the main goals of state and private placement agencies is to reunite children with their families whenever safely possible and while there are opportunities for adoption, those opportunities are not guaranteed. There is a chance that the child or children you open your home to could be taken away from you and reunited with their previous family, even after a strong emotional bond has been developed.

**Long wait times** – Caseworkers are often overworked, so things can move slowly. It may seem like it takes forever to have paperwork filed or to hear back from agencies. You will need a lot of patience.

**Possible emotional and/or mental health issues** – Foster children may come from homes that were broken by death, divorce, drugs, sexual abuse, physical abuse, financial hardship or many other scenarios. Because of this, there is a possibility that they may have developed aggressive behavior or emotional insecurities that could disrupt your household.

**Possible medical issues** – There are many children in foster care with medical issues, developmental delays and/or physical disabilities. It is important that you fully understand how your life will be impacted if you decide to open your home to a child with special needs. You may need to take the child to frequent doctor visits, prepare special diets, administer medications or even make modifications to your home.

**Possible negative interactions with birthparents** – You may have interactions with a child's birthparents when you foster a child and these interactions may not always be positive. Also, keep in mind that even if you work with an LGBT-friendly agency, the child's birthparents and/ or family members may not be so accepting. They may even be openly antagonistic toward their child growing up with LGBT parents.

## Reasons Why People Choose **Surrogacy**

**Biological link** – Surrogacy makes it possible for one or both of the parents in a same-sex relationship to have a biological link with the baby. Of course, only one sperm from one male can fertilize an egg, so a gay couple will have to decide who donates or they could just mix their semen together and see whose sperm wins the race. Alternatively, if the sperm is used from one of the males and an egg is used from a relative of the other male, the child would have a biological connection to both males in a same-sex relationship. It may also be possible for a gay couple to have twins where one baby is biologically related to one father and the other baby is biologically related to the other father.

**Participation in the pregnancy journey** – When a couple chooses surrogacy, they have the opportunity to witness and be a part of the pregnancy journey. It's possible for them to be present for sonograms, the baby's first heartbeat and maybe even get to feel the baby kick if the surrogate is in agreement.

**Opportunity to be present during birth** – If your surrogate is comfortable with it and you want to be present during birth, you have that opportunity. You may also get the chance to take pictures, video or even cut the umbilical cord. Just try not to be one of those parents who faint in the delivery room.

**Medical history** – Egg and sperm donors complete medical history forms allowing the parents to be aware of the biological family's medical history. Keep in mind, if you choose anonymous egg and sperm donors, you will not know if there are medical updates with the biological family in the future.

**Smooth and harmonious experience** – All parties involved sign contracts in the beginning allowing for expectations to be set early on. While there are always exceptions to every rule, this normally makes for a smooth and harmonious experience for everyone involved.

## Surrogacy Challenges

**Not everyone approves of surrogacy** – Some people see surrogacy as "baby selling" or "buying a baby" because of the large sums of money that are exchanged for the service. While it's true that it's your decision on how you expand your own family, be aware that some people among your friends, family or social circles might not approve.

**Invasive procedures** – The surrogate will need to go through a lot of medically invasive procedures, which can sometimes be difficult and uncomfortable.

**Possible medical complications** – With surrogacy, it often takes multiple attempts to conceive and miscarriages are common with surrogate pregnancies. It is important that you speak with a medical professional to get a clear understanding of the potential medical complications that could arise.

**Financial cost** – Many people find that the surrogacy route is too expensive. When taking into consideration the cost of hiring a surrogate, possibly paying a portion of the surrogate mother's living expenses, the cost of the medical procedures, agency fees, lawyer fees and more, you're looking at somewhere over $100,000. On top of that, many insurance companies won't cover the costs of the fertilization or delivery when using a surrogate.

**Possible legal complications** – Traditional surrogacy (the egg donor and surrogate are the same person) is currently treated the same as a birthmother placing her child for adoption, because there is a biological connection between the surrogate and the child. This could complicate things if the surrogate changes her mind and decides she wants parental rights. Because of this, all states currently prohibit traditional surrogacy agreements.

**Possible breach of contract** – Even though all parties sign a contract in the beginning, it is still possible for a surrogate to violate her end of the agreement. There is a risk the birthmother could voluntarily have an abortion without the consent of the intended parents or refuse to have an agreed-upon abortion when recommended by the physician. It is also possible that the surrogate could use drugs, consume alcohol or fail to follow other behavioral restrictions laid out in the contract.

**Scams** – Unfortunately, a simple online search brings up numerous surrogacy scam examples where agencies have run off with client funds and/ or closed their doors without giving notice, abandoning their clients in the process. Make sure you research potential agencies thoroughly prior to working with one and seek the advice of an independent attorney who can oversee the process and advocate on your behalf.

## Reasons Why People Choose **Assisted Reproduction**

**Biological connection** – There can be a biological link between the child and one of the women in a same-sex relationship if an egg from one of the women is used. There is also a possibility for both women to have a biological link with the child if the sperm donor is genetically linked to the non-biological mother.

**Shared contribution for lesbian couples** – Ovum sharing (or co-maternity) is an option that makes it possible for both women in a same-sex relationship to contribute to the conception of their child: One woman provides her egg and the other carries the baby. Some lesbian couples choose this option because both women in the relationship can contribute to the conception of their child.

**Being involved since inception** – Assisted reproduction gives you the benefit of being involved in your child's life from the moment he or she is conceived. You'll have the opportunity to see the sonogram and even listen to your child's first heartbeat. Women in same-sex relationships can support each other during the pregnancy journey by doing things like going to doctor visits and Lamaze classes together.

**Experiencing birth** – Assisted reproduction gives one of you the opportunity to carry and give birth to your child. If you are both in the same room during the actual delivery, a woman can support her partner by holding her hand and/or helping with breathing. She may even have the opportunity to cut the cord.

**More control** – If you or your partner decides to carry the baby, you will have a lot of control along the way, especially when it comes to what enters your body. You can choose whether or not to use prenatal vitamins, eat organic foods and refrain from using alcohol, drugs and tobacco.

## Assisted Reproduction Challenges

**Lack of insurance coverage** – Many insurance companies will not cover alternative insemination unless there is a diagnosis of "infertility" or if you have tried to inseminate without success for a period of time. Make sure you ask your health insurance company how they define infertility, what treatments are covered and if their policy covers insemination for same-sex couples.

**Cost** – For women who use a sperm bank, costs can add up depending on what services they use. Because many insurance companies won't cover assisted reproduction without a diagnosis of infertility, the journey can get expensive quickly.

**No guarantee of success** – There are no guarantees that one of you will become pregnant after going through assisted reproduction treatments. You could wind up trying multiple times, which could become very costly.

**Inconvenient facility locations** – Cryobanks are not in every city and you may not have a local clinic near you. This can make things difficult when you have to arrange multiple doctor visits.

**Changes to your body** – If you choose to get pregnant, you will also experience some of the changes to your body that come with pregnancy, such as weight gain, aches, pains, stretch marks, spider veins, additional body hair, acne and more.

**Difficult feelings** – While this doesn't always happen, sometimes a woman can start to develop feelings of jealousy when she is not the one carrying the baby. She may feel that she is missing out on parts of the experience and this could add strain to the relationship. Because of this, sometimes women in same-sex relationships make a decision that they will take turns getting pregnant. Whatever you decide to do as a couple, open communication is key.

## Reasons Why People Choose **Known Donors**

**Relationship with your child** – As your child grows up, he or she can develop a relationship with the donor. Your child will have a better understanding of where he or she came from and why he or she might have certain characteristics and traits.

**Biological connection** – It is still possible for a child to have a biological connection to both women in a same-sex relationship if the sperm donor is genetically linked to the non-biological mother.

**Cost** – For women who choose not to get medical assistance, but instead get pregnant with the help of a friend, the cost is significantly lower.

# Known Donor Challenges

**Parental rights** – For women who become pregnant with the assistance of a known donor, there is greater risk that the donor may later try to claim parental rights. There may even be a possibility that you or your partner could lose custody. When using a known donor, it is recommended that you consult with an attorney and have a Known Donor Agreement signed. Keep in mind that a Known Donor Agreement will not necessarily terminate the donor's rights, even if it says so. That's why consulting an attorney beforehand is crucial, especially since the laws vary by state.

**Sexually transmitted diseases** – Using a known donor at home without testing has a similar risk to having unprotected sex in terms of sexually transmitted infections. If you are using a known donor, even if he looks 100 percent healthy, consider having him tested through a sperm bank or fertility clinic. Testing will also inform you if the donor has a viable sperm count before you begin the process.

## Reasons Why People Choose Unknown Donors

**Reduced risk of custody challenges** – Unknown donors surrender all of their parenting rights when working with a sperm bank. Things are not always cut and dried with a known donor. Consult an attorney to understand the laws in your state.

**Reduced risk of problematic genes** – When using a sperm bank, you have access to the donor's comprehensive medical history. With this knowledge, you have the ability to control your child's exposure to problematic genes.

**Reduced risk of sexually transmitted diseases** – When using a sperm bank, specimens can be quarantined and tested for sexually transmitted diseases. This can reduce the risk of passing anything on to you or your child.

## Unknown Donor Challenges

**Relationship with the child** – Typically, your child will not have the opportunity to know the donor. Sometimes, donors will agree to have their identity revealed once the child turns eighteen. Your child may have a yearning to know more about his or her full biological heritage.

**Unknown future medical history** – If you choose an unknown donor, there is a high chance that you will not know of any changes in the donor family's medical history. It can be stressful if your child becomes sick and the sperm bank is unable or unwilling to find the donor to provide clues.

**Frozen sperm can be less effective** – Frozen sperm will not live as long as fresh sperm. Because of the frozen sperm's shorter lifespan, the timing of the insemination needs to be much more precise.

## Reasons Why People Choose **Co-Parenting**

**Additional support** – When you choose to co-parent, you're not going through the journey alone and you can utilize the support of your co-parenting partners when difficult situations arise.

**Balance** – Because more people are involved in raising the child, there are many opportunities to create a more balanced life. While one parent or couple is taking care of the child, the other person or couple can catch up on things like sleep, chores, work-related activities and hobbies. This allows you to be more focused on your child when he or she is present.

**Flexibility** – Because there is shared custody, you can have flexible time while your child is staying with his or her other parents. Because of this, it's easier to schedule date nights and have more personal alone time with your partner.

**Sharing expenses** – When two sets of parents are raising a child, if each of them is working, there will be four incomes to help with the expenses of raising a child. This can alleviate a lot of financial stress if it is clear upfront how each person is going to contribute.

**Biological connection** – For some people, having a biological connection with their child is important. In a co-parenting situation, it is possible for both biological parents to take active roles in raising the child.

**Participation in the pregnancy journey** – Everyone involved has the opportunity to witness and be a part of the pregnancy journey. It can be possible for them to be present for sonograms, the baby's first heartbeat and more.

**Opportunity to be present during birth** – If everyone is comfortable with it and the doctors allow it, each of you can be present during birth. You may also get the chance to take photos or video and even cut the umbilical cord.

## Co-Parenting Challenges

**Different rules and parenting styles** – If the moms have one set of rules at their house and the dads have another set of rules at theirs, things can get pretty complicated very quickly. Making sure everyone is on the same page in the beginning will make things easier down the road.

**Proximity** – It may not seem like an issue in the beginning, but if the other couple (or person) you co-parent with lives a fair distance away, this could eventually turn into a major inconvenience. Some people choose to live very close to each other or even in the same home to avoid this.

**Holidays** – It may not always be possible for everyone to be together during the holidays. Consider how this will impact you and your children. Keep in mind, extended family members may be disappointed with not being together during these times, too. Again, as with everything else, setting clear expectations with holiday schedules upfront will make things a lot easier.

**A move could complicate things** – What if one of you has to move to another city, state or country for work or other reasons? This could complicate your joint custody plans.

# APPENDIX C

## Questions to Ask

### Before Choosing **Open Adoption**

1. How important is biological heritage to your family plan?

2. Are you comfortable having ongoing contact with your child's birthparents? If so, how much contact are you comfortable with?

3. Are you comfortable with the fact that even though you will know who the birthmother is, there is a chance that the birthfather will be unknown?

4. Can you afford open adoption? If so, where will you draw the line with adoption-related expenses? While open adoption is not the most expensive route, it is important to understand that in addition to agency fees, there may be other unexpected costs that can accrue, such as third-party agency fees and birthmother living expenses. These things add up, so make sure you get a full cost breakdown upfront and provide yourself a hefty cushion.

5. How comfortable are you with being publicly visible? When you create a birthmother letter, you will probably be creating an online profile so birthparents can find you. Your personal information (pictures,

relationship status, hobbies and any other information you disclose) will likely show up in online search engines.

6. Are there any reasons you would choose not to match with a birthmother?

7. How will you and your partner deal with the waiting period?

8. If you are an unmarried couple and you live in a state where only one of you is allowed to adopt in the beginning, which one of you will that be and how will you ensure that everyone in your family is legally protected?

9. Is your job flexible enough to work around your open adoption journey? You may need to travel to another state at a moment's notice when the birthmother goes into labor. Also, you may need to stay in that state until all paperwork is processed and you are cleared to leave. There is no set timeframe for this, so flexibility is important.

10. How will it impact you and your family if you suddenly lose contact with your child's birthparents sometime after birth?

## Before Choosing **Foster Care**

1. Are you only interested in temporary placements or is your goal to have a placement that will lead to a permanent adoption?

2. What age child is ideal for you and your partner and what ages are you willing to accept?

3. Are you open to adopting a sibling group?

4. Are you comfortable opening your home to a child with physical disabilities and/or emotional issues?

5. Are you and your partner in agreement on standards of discipline and how to implement those standards?

6. Are you comfortable with the possibility that you may be interacting with the child's birthparents?

7. Do you have the emotional agility to simultaneously act as a support system for a birthparent who is trying to rectify his or her behaviors

and reunify with his or her children, while also bonding with the child as a potential permanent parent should those reunification efforts fail?

8. Are you willing and prepared to advocate for the needs of your child within a public school system and get appropriate educational support?

9. If your adoptive child is of a different ethnicity than yourself and your partner, how will you create an environment where he or she is educated about and connected to his or her birth heritage?

10. Do your family and friends support your decision to move forward with foster care?

## Before Choosing **Surrogacy**

1. Is a biological connection with your child important to you or your partner?

2. Do you have the financial means to pay for surrogacy and can you realistically afford it?

3. For males, will you or your partner be providing the sperm and if so, how will you decide who does? For females, will you or your partner be providing the egg and if so, how will you decide who does?

4. Do you prefer that the donor is someone you know or do you prefer that they remain anonymous?

5. If one of you has a biological connection to the child and the other does not, how will this impact the non-biological parent emotionally?

6. How much contact do you want with your surrogate during pregnancy?

7. If you find out there is a complication with the fetus during pregnancy, what will you do and are you and your partner on the same page about this? Make sure your surrogate is on the same page as well.

8. What role (if any) will the surrogate or donor have in your child's life after birth?

9. What role (if any) will the extended family members of the surrogate or donor have in your child's life?

10. How many children are you hoping to have and are you open to a twin or triplet pregnancy if permitted by the treating physician and agreed to by the surrogate?

## Before Choosing **Assisted Reproduction**

1. Is a biological connection with your child important to you or your partner?

2. How important is it for you or your partner to have the experience of being pregnant?

3. Are you comfortable with the various medical tests and procedures that you will have to go through?

4. Which type of donor are you more comfortable with, a known donor or an unknown one?

5. If you choose a known donor, are you comfortable with the donor playing a role in the child's life? Whatever your answer is to this question and no matter how much you trust the donor, always consult an attorney and make sure you understand the legal implications of your decision in the state where you live.

6. What offspring limits are you comfortable with? Each sperm bank will have its own policy on donor limits, so make sure you understand what they are. It could be the difference between your child having ten siblings or over one hundred!

7. What happens if your sperm donor fathers another child later in life?

8. Will you be using the eggs from one of you in the relationship or will you be using a donor's eggs? If you decide to use your own eggs, how does this make your partner feel, knowing that you will be biologically related to the child while she will not be or vice versa?

9. Who will carry the baby?

10. How will you discuss donor insemination with your child?

## Before Choosing **Co-Parenting**

1. If your co-parenting situation will involve more than two people, who will be providing the sperm and egg?

2. Will you be utilizing the services of a reproduction center or will you be using a DIY approach?

3. Have you taken into consideration that the person or people with whom you are going to co-parent may have extended family members who will want to be involved in the child's life?

4. What will the living situation be for the child? Whom will he or she live with and when?

5. How will holidays work within your family structure?

6. Who will make major decisions for the child such as healthcare and schooling?

7. How will finances be handled? For example, will you all share financial responsibility for everything (medical, food, clothes, education, school supplies, extracurricular activities, etc.) or will certain people be responsible for certain aspects?

8. How will you explain your co-parenting situation to your child and to other people?

9. What if one of the parents needs to move to a different city or state?

10. What happens if one of you violates the agreement? It is highly recommended that you consult with an attorney when creating a co-parenting agreement. This way everyone can be on the same page and there will be a clear understanding about what will happen if someone breaks the agreement.